# Alternative Perspectives on School Improvement

David Hopkins & Marvin Wideen
*Simon Fraser University*

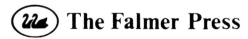

**The Falmer Press**

A member of the Taylor & Francis Group
London and New York

**UK**  The Falmer Press, Falmer House, Barcombe, Lewes, East Sussex, BN8 5DL

**USA**  The Falmer Press, Taylor & Francis Inc., 242 Cherry Street, Philadelphia, PA 19106-1906

First published in 1984

**Library of Congress Cataloging in Publication Data**

Main entry under title:

Alternative perspectives on school improvement.

Includes bibliographies and index.
1. School management and organization—Addresses, essays, lectures. 2. Educational innovations—Addresses, essays, lectures. 3. Teachers—In-service training—Addresses, essays, lectures. 4. Curriculum planning—Addresses, essays, lectures. I. Hopkins, David. II. Wideen, Marvin.
LB2806.A527  1984  371.2  83-25497
ISBN 0-905273-82-6
ISBN 0-905273-81-8 (pbk.)

Jacket design by Leonard Williams

Typeset in 11/13 Garamond
by Imago Publishing Ltd., Thame, Oxon.

*Printed in Great Britain by Taylor & Francis (Printers) Ltd, Basingstoke*

# Contents

# Contents

*To Mary and Loretta*

# Introduction: Alternative Perspectives on School Improvement

Jacob Getzels once asked, 'How can schools be improved?' and then answered his own question: 'In almost every conceivable way known to man.' [quoted in Schmuck, R., and Miles, M. (1971), p. 14.] In the face of such a salutary prognosis it may appear presumptuous to produce a book on school improvement. Yet the book is timely, and for at least two reasons. First, the topic itself – school improvement – is becoming increasingly important, given economic restraints and the recognition that the school is the essential unit of change in the educational system. Second, the presuppositions underlying these essays appreciate the individual response to complex societal situations, and as such are vital to the regeneration and reconceptualization of teaching and learning. A common theme throughout the book is that schools can best be improved by re-examining the nature of teaching, by emphasizing and building on the uniqueness and diversity of teachers, and by appreciating the culture from which and in which teaching and learning occur. As such, the book provides an alternative view to the centralized prescriptive mode of school improvement currently maintained in many jurisdictions and prevalent in much educational thought; and which failed to meet its promise in the sixties and seventies.

School improvement is a generic term that we use to refer to those developmental efforts which focus on the school. As such, school improvement encompasses topics such as in-service, the professional development of teachers, the implementation of education innovation, school focused curriculum development, organization development, and the roles of administrators, teachers and students in knowledge utilization.

This book is the result of a collective and sustained dialogue by the authors around the theme of school improvement. The occasion for this dialogue was a Summer Institute on Teacher Education (SITE) concerning 'Strategies for School Improvement' held at Simon Fraser University, Vancouver, Canada during the Summer of 1980. The participants in the institute were invited not solely because of their reputation, but also for their particular perspective on school improvement. So, for instance, Ted Aoki's concern with curriculum implementation and evaluation complemented Lawrence Stenhouse's vision of the teacher as curriculum developer and researcher, which again contrasted with Jean Rudduck's emphasis on the pupil perspective in change efforts; and so on. As a result, the seminars to which they contributed, and the resulting papers which form the basis of the book provide a coherent set of perspectives on school improvement. As the Institute progressed, it became evident that despite differing areas of expertise, the group as a whole shared a common philosophy and approach to schooling which was somewhat different from the contemporary norm. The discovery of this common bond challenged the group, and encouraged careful attention to and critique of each other's work. The result is a coherent collection of original papers which reflect different aspects of how schools can be improved, but which are characterized by a single purpose and philosophy. This also explains the reference to each other's work and to the SITE lectures that are contained in the following chapters.

We have described the setting from which the book emerged, because it highlights a number of its important features. First, most of the essays are original contributions written at the same time and in conjunction with each other. As a result they represent a unified and coherent message which has not been previously published. Second, each of the authors writes from a perspective which is grounded in rich experience, and which has the benefit of hindsight. The chapters by Schmuck and Runkel for instance, reflect fourteen years of experimentation, research and theory building in organizational change in schools. The ideas of and Lawrence Stenhouse Jean Rudduck were first developed in the crucible of the Humanities Curriculum Project in the late sixties, and further refined in their work at the Centre for Applied Research in Education. Similarly, Bruce Joyce's reputation as a teacher educator; Ted Aoki's contribution to curriculum development in Canada; Michael Fullan's writings on educational change, and all well known and based on field experience. Third, the book speaks to and is written about practitioners, teachers, administrators and students. Those attending the institute included a wide range of educators but consisted mainly of teachers and persons responsible for curriculum development and in-service programmes. Thus, the presentations were criticized by an audience close to the action in schools. The contents of the book reflect this critical analysis.

After the manuscript had been prepared, the publishers suggested the addition of extra material to reinforce the international flavour of the book. We turned to our colleagues in Australia, New Zealand and Sweden; and are grateful of Ken Eltis, Viviane Robinson and Mats Eckholm for sending us chapters at short notice. The issues raised in their essays are complementary to the theme of the book, and we are pleased with the opportunity to provide a wider perspective.

The book is divided into four sections. The first – the concept of school improvement – attempts to set some parameters around the concept of school improvement. In an introductory chapter David Hopkins reviews the major theme of the book and sketches out the domain of school improvement. By way of contrast, Richard Schmuck, operationalizes the concept, first by reviewing various themes that give credibility to the school improvement concept and then by describing an ideal model of the autonomous school. Mats Eckholm grounds the concept in a practical reality, by describing some school improvement initiatives that have occurred in Sweden.

The second section – the actors – focuses on the individuals involved in the school improvement process. The section opens with a chapter on the neglected user in the change process – the student. Here Jean Rudduck argues for the importance of considering the student's role in innovation. In the following chapter Lawrence Stenhouse uses the metaphor of the artist to highlight the teacher's responsibility for developing and sustaining his or her own competence. Bruce Joyce and Beverly Showers extend this theme by describing ways in which teachers can acquire, improve and maintain their teaching skills through peer coaching. Finally in this section, Michael Fullan examines the role of the principal as a change agent and gatekeeper for school improvement efforts.

The third section 'Perspectives on Change' contains four papers that review different approaches to school improvement. Ted Aoki in criticizing the normative approach to curriculum implementation proposes a view of implementation as praxis, and in so doing provides a rationale for the alternative approach to school improvement taken in this book. Ken Eltis and his colleagues writing from a similar perspective describes ways in which the continuing education of teachers can contribute to school improvement. School based review is an important aspect of school improvement, and in her chapter Viviane Robinson analyzes the idea in the context of New Zealand. In the section's final chapter Philip Runkel together with Richard Schmuck describe organization development as a change strategy that schools can use (with a little help) to improve themselves.

The final section is a 'call to action.' If the previous sections of the book have discussed the nature of school improvement efforts, this section is a challenge to operationalize and implement those ideas. In his chapter 'Maintaining diversity in schools' Philip Runkel makes an impassioned plea for the maintenance of diversity and the encouragement of individuality in and within schools. Finally Marvin Wideen and Ian Andrews in their chapter 'Implications for Practice' reflect on the issues raised in the book and point to ways in which they can be utilized within a typical (your?) school setting.

Describing the sections and chapters of the book in this way may be misleading, for it could imply a hierarchial ordering, a linear progression, or a tidy conceptual analysis. None of these apply because, as will be seen later, school improvement efforts if they are to be at all successful or worthwhile are neither hierarchical, linear, nor contrived. School improvement, in the way it is described in this book, implies people collectively taking responsibility for their actions and working hard, very hard, together.

### Reference

SCHMUCK, R.A. and MILES, M.B. (Eds) (1971) *Organization Development in Schools*, La Jolla, California, University Associates.

# Section One:
## The Concept of School Improvement

*School improvement is a nebulous term, and one that requires clarification. The three chapters in this section take this as their task.* **David Hopkins** *in the initial chapter sketches out the territory of school improvement, by identifying constituent elements and pointing to recent developments. He also clarifies and articulates the 'alternative perspective' that characterize the essays in this book.* **Richard Schmuck** *approaches the same task from a different angle, and takes as his focus the concept of the autonomous school. From his description Schmuck develops properties and characteristics which provide an ideal model of the school that is consistent with the issues and themes raised later in the book. By way of contrast to these somewhat theoretical discussions,* **Mats Eckholm** *in his chapter reviews the experience of a number of school improvement efforts in Sweden. In doing he adds texture and reality to the concept. Indeed, the main purpose of these three chapters is to provide a context and ground work for what follows.*

# What is School Improvement? Staking Out the Territory

David Hopkins
Simon Fraser University

It is appropriate that an initial chapter in a book such as this should map out in broad terms the field of endeavour which is the sum of the subsequent individual contributions. This is particularly important when considering the topic of school improvement, for the concept is at present diffuse and slippery. But there is an even more important task to be accomplished in this chapter. We have claimed for the book the title of 'alternative perspectives . . .', and, in the introduction, alluded to a common theme that characterizes the following pages. So the twofold purpose of this chapter is not only to stake out the territory of school improvement but also to clarify the perspective that the book takes on this topic. I have chosen to do the latter task first.

One theme that characterizes the essays in this book is their reaction to the norms of contemporary western educational thought. These norms have been engendered by the dominance of a philosophic orientation predicated on instrumental reason, which in turn is based on scientism and technology. Aoki (1979) has called this way of thinking the empirical-analytic paradigm and his distinction between this orientation and phenomenology and critical theory is grounded in the work of Jurgen Habermas. In *Knowledge and Human Interests* Habermas (1972) outlines a tri-paradigmatic framework which describes the variety of actions that we as humans can engage in. Aoki argues that the North American educational system is imbued with the values associated with the empirical analytic tradition, to the exclusion of values epitomized by the phenomenological or critical theoretic paradigms.

The roots of the empirical analytic paradigm, which appear to pervade most aspects of North American life if one is to take seriously the radical critiques which flowered during the seventies, need not concern us here. Of more immediate interest are the manifestations of this tendency and the values implicit in them. The values most closely associated with this philosophic attitude are those which value control, efficiency, predictability and accountability. Understanding is in terms of facts, knowing is predicated on empiricism, and explanations are based on causal, functional or hypothetico-deductive reasons. Knowledge itself is regarded as facts, or generalizations from cause and effect laws. The emphasis on knowledge forms of this type is reflected in a characteristic attitude to life – one that regards it with certainty and predictability – and considers that reality is a given.

The impact of this way of thinking on the educational system is as deep rooted as it is ubiquitous. The basic organization of schools – age grades, didactic instruction, centrally imposed curricula, hierarchical structuring of personnel, elaborate and artificial codes of behavior – all reflect a linear, mechanistic and deterministic view of teaching and learning. In addition schools, in a functionally structured society like ours, assume a major reproductive role. As agents of cultural transmission it is unsurprising, therefore, to find them organized on an industrial model. Means are clearly subjugated to ends, and the ends themselves are arbitrarily determined by a pragmatic functional analysis of contemporary society. Staying with the industrial metaphor, society determines the nature of student outcomes and the schools consequently engage administrators, teachers, and students in a process designed to achieve that level of productivity. As a result, education becomes a linear, easily controlled and evaluated process. Schools are environments designed specifically for productivity, and teachers are relegated to the role of mechanics, implementing standardized treatments on the students who enter the process as a raw product and emerge as an approximation to society's ideal.

On a day-to-day basis I am certain that we all encounter incidents which fit well with that characterization. An example from the curriculum field may help to further explicate the argument. The failure of the curriculum reform movement is a clear indictment of a centralized and linear approach to curriculum development. The post-sputnik flurry led to massive investment in education, which manifested itself in attempts at improvement through curriculum innovation. The curriculum reform movement, despite the blaze of publicity, the glossy, colourful and imaginative products, dramatically failed to alter life in schools. As Schmuck and Miles (1971:1) commented,

schools remained largely as they were, with new features . . .
in evidence only here and there.

Production was excellent, diffusion was okay, but witness the
unopened or partly rifled packages of material in school stockrooms,
and then one begins to realize the reasons for the failure. Top-down
or linear approaches to change which ignore the user do not work:
irrespective of this fact, linear or centralized models of change are still
the predominant mode of delivery.

If this book is a reaction to the contemporary empirical analytic
perspective, what is the alternative view? I have already referred to
the phenomenological and critical theoretic paradigms, and it is these
modes of thinking and action that best characterize the forms of
teaching and learning advocated in this book. In his essay on
curriculum implementation, Ted Aoki refers to the contemporary
and prevailing ideology as instrumental action, and contrasts it to the
notion of practical action or praxis. Praxis implies a negotiation
between object and subject which results in a meaningful but
unpredictable outcome. Under the prevalent mode of learning a
student is subject to a curriculum in order to meet some prespecified
objective. Praxis, on the other hand, implies that students interact
with the curriculum in order to extract some subjective meaning from
it, in an attempt to broaden or deepen their intellectual perspective
which may or may not be amenable to pre-specification. For as
Stenhouse (1975:82) remarks:

> Education as induction into knowledge is successful to the
> extent that it makes the behavioural outcomes of the students
> unpredictable.

Bruce Joyce in his SITE lecture commented on the state of the
art of educational change, and maintained that despite the considerable technical expertise developed in this area, little of this technology
is effectively changing schools. What is needed, he said, are more
'wild-eyed crazies'. People who have the vision and the energy to
mobilize and use this technological understanding in creative ways.
What has been devalued and ignored is the human element. The
creativity and uniqueness that belongs to us all needs to be incorporated within the ambit of school improvement strategies and
theories.

It is this generalized theme that re-occurs throughout the book
in various guises. Aoki refers to critical venturing, Stenhouse uses
the metaphor of teacher as artist, Schmuck and Runkel refer to

schools as imagining systems and so on – but the underlying thread is the authenticity of the relationship between subject and object with the assumption that it possesses integrity and uniqueness. By implication it is these qualities that are inhibited, dulled, and even extinguished when the parameters of cause and effect, certainty of outcome, and control are placed around them.

To recapitulate: with reference to Habermas' tri-paradigmatic framework, our critique of the contemporary educational system is focused on the manifestation of values implicit in the empirical analytic tradition. These values which emphasize control, accountability, certainty and predictability, result in an educational system which militates against uniqueness, creativity and individual autonomy. Implicit in these essays is a belief that more emphasis on communication, on appreciating subjective meaning, and on critical reflection will improve the quality of schooling. While it would be a misrepresentation to claim that this book reflects a clearly thought out phenomenological or critical stance, what is true is that the various essays collected here make an argument for values espoused by these paradigms, in contrast to the pervasive and ubiquitous empirical analytic tradition that currently characterizes the educational system.

Having described the philosophic presupposition on which the book is based, I now want to discuss in more detail the reasons why school improvement is a pressing issue, and to identify the targets of school improvement efforts.

John Nisbet (1973:18–19), commenting on the term 'creativity of the school', (which has the same sense as the phrase 'school improvement') defines it as the:

> capacity to adopt, adapt, generate or reject innovations . . . It implies a flexibility of approach which has three elements: confronting problems, responding to problems and evaluating the response to problems.

Nisbet is saying that the school (that is, school personnel) needs to become more pro-active, responsible and autonomous, and to take more control over its (their) actions. One is used to hearing the Rogerian phrase – the fully functioning person; the autonomous or creative school is the systemic educational equivalent of this humanistic idea. This school is not one that is necessarily progressive, radical or conservative, there are no values implicit in the term; what is implied, is an organization that is self-determining, and has the capacity to deal with its environment, as well as responding to the needs of its members.

But why the school? Why focus on that as the unit of development, particularly in relatively centralized educational systems? There are a number of reasons, but three in particular stand out; the failure of the curriculum reform movement, the failure of post-industrial societies to maintain sustained growth in the gross national product (GNP), and the current ubiquity of social change.

The failure of the curriculum reform movement has already been discussed. In hindsight, the major lesson to be drawn from this experience is that top down approaches to change do not work; for, as in this instance, the centre-periphery model of educational change proved itself conspicuously and expensively inadequate. Recent work on curriculum implementation (Fullan and Pomfret, 1977) implies that for the change to be effective the locus of control needs to be shifted much closer to the nexus of educational interactions – the school.

The inability of the West to sustain economic growth and the spectre of the steady erosion of natural resources has, in the last decade, dramatically affected the educational system. So much so that the arguments put forward by Illich (1971) in *Deschooling Society*, appear today, a decade later, to be almost prophetic. Faced with low or even negative economic growth it becomes increasingly difficult to sustain the educational machine at its present level. This societal problem has been exacerbated in education by recent changes in the demographic balance that has resulted in declining enrolments in many Western schools. These changes have had two major results. First, faced with static or decreased budgets, school districts find themselves in little more than a maintenance mode. With money so scarce, enhanced quality becomes more and more the responsibility of the school. Because schools cannot go elsewhere for help they are forced to turn in upon themselves and to garner their own resources. Second, declining enrolments have resulted in a static and aging teaching population. This increases the need for the school to be more responsible for staff development, because no longer can it rely on an infusion of new blood to generate enthusiasm.

Against this scenario of economic decline must be set the social milieu in which it is occurring. And it is one of pervasive and rampant social change. Change as ubiquitous as we are now experiencing tends to create a paranoia which manifests itself in a compulsive desire to keep abreast of the change. Perversely, this creates an alienation stemming from the inability of the individual to control the change. The implication of this for schools is that, as society's major agent of socialization, there is pressure on them to reflect these changes and to be able to relate teaching methods, classroom climate and curricula to changing societal norms. At the same time they have a responsibility to the communities they serve, for school is the major societal institution intervening in most people's lives. Potentially, as Bruce Joyce (1978) has demonstrated in the Urban/Rural Project, schools can significantly reduce the sense of alienation and anomie individuals and communities increasingly feel. Unfortunately this is rarely the case.

These three arguments – the failure of the curriculum reform movement, decreasing resources and the ubiquity of social change – argue powerfully for the consideration of the school as the prime unit of change within the educational system. They also determine the character of school improvement efforts. The failure of the curriculum reform movement argues for innovation emanating from, or at least being mediated through, the local level. It also supports the case for school-based curriculum development. The reduction in natural resources, the decline in the GNP and the recent demographic changes create a need for schools that can sustain and develop themselves without the consistent injection of outside resources, and also for a teaching force that becomes increasingly resonsible for its own professional development. The ubiquity of social change argues for a responsive and autonomous school which is sensitive to the needs of its immediate environment. If these characteristics are isolated, the resulting list gives one a feel for the scope of school improvement. It implies a school which takes more responsibility for: the development of its own curriculum; the professional development of its staff; innovation and change; its own development (that is, self-renewing and organizationally healthy); and the wider society which it reflects and the community which it serves. At this point it may be worth sketching out in a little more detail what is implied by these topics and the interrelationship between them, for they comprise the substance of school improvement.

First, consider the relationship between curriculum development and in-service teacher education. Aspects of the curriculum reform movement have already been discussed: its failure to affect practice substantially has encouraged educational researchers and curriculum developers to examine more closely the concept of curriculum implementation. The plethora of recent papers on implementation gives fair warning of the complexity and difficulty associated with introducing new ideas into the educational milieu. Fullan and Pomfret (1977) suggest that there are five components associated with the implementation of new curriculum. These involve: one, the production of new materials; two, structural changes to accommodate changes in practice; three, role or behaviour change on the part of administrators, teachers, and the acceptance of such by pupils; four, a knowledge and understanding of the materials and processes involved in change by all those concerned; and five, a valuing of the endeavour by the principal actors involved. Obviously this is a much more sophisticated process than just naively sending a package of materials to a school – and it has a number of implications. First, that the teacher in the classroom occupies a pivotal role in the implementation process and, second, that effective curriculum development requires in-service training. Analysis of this type ridicules the pretentions of some curriculum developers who claim to have produced teacher-proof materials!

If this argument is accepted then it follows that the school should have more responsibility for curriculum development. Despite the prevalent myth that the articulation of general performance objectives by a central authority precludes innovation in the classroom, it needs to be realized that the specification of a core curriculum does not inhibit pedagogy. While the central authority may lay down what to teach, they typically leave the 'how' of education to the teacher. For example, the British Columbia Ministry of Education Curriculum Planning Document states (1979:3).

> that while the Ministry specifies learning outcomes and prescribes basic textbooks, the most important task is left to the classroom teacher: the task of deciding how a skill or concept is to be taught to each student or group of students.

By taking this position the Ministry sanctions the teachers' involvement in curriculum development, and implicitly encourages them to nurture and develop their own competence. This line of argument speaks directly to the curriculum development in-service interface, because the only system support for continuing development and enhanced competence is through in-service and professional development.

Besides being improtant aspects of school improvement, in-service curriculum development and implementation are also facets of process of planned change. This includes changes in individuals, in curriculum, and the process of change itself. A goal of school improvement is an ability to handle change.

Two observations are worth making here about planned change:

the first is that change is difficult to achieve. The difficulty increases with the degree of complexity of the change; the more complex the change, the more the need to coordinate the actions of more people and the more the need to change the assumptions and norms that they hold. Schools are open systems and are influenced by their environment, but they are also more than that. Runkel and his colleagues (1979) make the point that schools are comprised of individuals who all have unique images of themselves and their schools; as a result schools as entities possess images of these images. This notion of the school as an imagining system adds enormously to the difficulty of our conceptualization of institutional change. It heightens if not parodies the point that the system in which we are intervening requires as careful consideration as the object of change itself.

The second observation is that in instances of successful change the object of change itself changes. Identical innovations assume different characteristics in different settings. This is what Berman and McLaughlin (1977) have called mutual adaptation. The innovation itself changes to meet the unique set of circumstances within the school, and the school changes as a result of the intervention. During this process of mutual adaptation the school gradually gains ownership of the innovation as the individuals adapt it to fit their needs and assimilate it as part of their personal repertoire of behaviours.

These two observations reflect the dialectic between individual and systemic change. Emrick and Peterson (1978:53) made a similar point in their synthesis of five major studies of educational change when they wrote,

> From these study findings it appears there are two separate but parallel dimensions to this change process: a personal dimension which involves the change process occurring within individuals (cognitive, behavioural, affective) as they acquire and make use of new knowledge, and a systemic dimension, which involves the concomitant changes occurring in the user environment (organizational, social, political). Furthermore, these separate but parallel processes appear to unfold as interdependent stages, both within and across dimensions.

Against this analysis of change there is a further dimension to consider. The healthy, positive and growthful interactions needed for effective change, in-service, curriculum development and implementation, can only occur within systems or subsystems which have high productivity, high quality of life and an organizational capacity to solve their own problems. This means that the systemic properties of the school are of paramount importance in any self-improvement effort as they determine the quality of life therein. Many potentially powerful educational reforms have floundered because little attention was given to the organizational context in which they were to occur. Any change has to be considered against the culture in which it intervenes.

The introduction of a new grading system by a teacher in her own classroom (while perhaps important to her and her students) is much easier to implement than, say, a principal's decision to adopt a centres approach throughout the elementary school. In the latter instance not only does the physical manifestation of the change have to occur, but also a concomitant change in the norms, social relations and communication patterns of the school. Schmuck (in Nisbet, 1973:109) puts it this way:

> While in-service education has sometimes successfully brought about changes in the individual teacher, it has not tended to help teachers develop the sorts of communication and problem-solving norms and skills that would increase their adaptability as an organizational unit. This is where organization development comes in. Organization development (abbreviated as OD) is a planned and sustained effort to apply behavioural science to system improvement, using reflexive, self-analytic methods.

The emphasis in OD is on the system or group rather than the individual, and its technology is aimed at having organization members themselves:

> examine current difficulties and their causes and participate actively in the reformation of goals, the development of new group process skills, the redesign of structures and procedures for achieving the goals, the alteration of the working climate of the school and the assessment of results.

The goal of OD is to create a capacity within the school for problem solving; to have the activities mentioned above as commonplace and acceptable. This implies that the four components of a problem-solving capacity – the meta skills – as Runkel and Schmuck (see section three, page 155) call them (viz., diagnosis, searching for resources, mobilizing synergistic action, and monitoring) are institutionalized within the school's organizational norms. It is a similar idea to Nisbet's 'adopt, adapt, generate or reject innovations' and provides a necessary but not sufficient definition of the goal of school improvement efforts.

In this brief tour around the territory of school improvement, I have argued that the organizational health of a school is related to its attitude towards planned change, curriculum development, in-service, and the role of the teacher in the classroom. The interdependence of these elements, the dialectic emanating from their interaction and the philosophy of education which they espouse, gives a vitality and importance to the topic of school improvement.

The territory of school improvement is a dynamic one. Much has happened since this book was conceptualized to define and etch more clearly the landscape of school improvement. For example, the findings of several research projects initiated in the mid/late seventies have been disseminated and become part of the conventional wisdom, thereby increasing the level of awareness towards school improvement (Lehming and Kane 1981, Fullan 1982). A number of major school improvement initiatives have occurred, such as the Dutch Autonomous School project (Van Velzen, 1979), the school improvement programs in California and New York (David, 1982) and the current emphasis of school based evaluation in Britain and Australia (Hopkins, 1983). In addition, the Organization for Economic and Cultural Development (OECD) has recently begun a major International School Improvement Project (Bolam, 1982; Van Velzen, 1982). Let me briefly review some of these occurrences, and see what they add to the concept and territory of school improvement.

There is an increasing awareness of the problem of educational change and school reform. The experience of the sixties and seventies has led to a more reflective attitude towards change and this is evident in much recent writing. As Fullan (1982) says:

> It is only in the last twelve years (since about 1970) that we have come to understand how educational change works in practice. In the 1960s educators were busy developing and introducing reforms. In the 1970s they were busy failing at putting them into practice. Out of this rather costly endeavor (psychologically and financially) has come a strong base of evidence about how and why educational reform fails or succeeds.

This evidence enables contemporary school improvement efforts to proceed perhaps more cautiously, but with more certainty of success. Similarly, Lehming and Kane's (1981) recent book contains a series of papers that review state-of-the art research on educational dissemination and change at the school level. These papers address topics such as the organizational features of schools, work incentives for school personnel, the role of principals and external consultants, and the problem of implementation. Work such as this, as the editors say, is vitally important in laying the groundwork for a new generation of research and policy in the area. Bruce Joyce remarked in his SITE lecture that we have reached a plateau of understanding concerning the process of educational change. We now have to experiment with implementation to find the right combination of approaches. The contemporary literature increasingly provides guidelines for these endeavours.

Examples of such experimentation are widespread. In the chapter that follows, Richard Schmuck briefly describes a Dutch project aimed at developing an autonomous school and Van Velzen (1979) discusses this programme in detail. The program was a major national attempt to improve schools by granting them more autonomy and creating both internal and external support facilities for the development and institutionalisation of the concept. In her paper, 'School based strategies: Implications for government policy' Jane David (1982) suggests that there will be increased emphasis on school based strategies for educational change, and describes four assumptions upon which such strategies are based (David 1982:1–2):

> One assumption is that change does not occur unless the particulars of a school and its context are taken into account. A second is that school staff will not be committed to a change effort unless they have had the opportunity to be involved in decisions concerning the shape of this project. A third is that effective schools are characterized by a school-wide focus – a set of shared goals and a unified approach to instruction as opposed to several separate, uncoordinated projects and approaches. Finally, proponents of school-based strategies believe that any planning effort that encourages self-awareness and reflection on the part of school staff will greatly increase the chances that behaviors will change.

These assumptions are consistent with the ideas already discussed in this chapter and which are taken up by other contributors in the rest of the book. What is of particular interest is David's review of school improvement projects in California and New York that have been based on these assumptions. A similar emphasis on school development is reflected in the current interest in school based evaluation that is evident in a number of OECD countries. Although many school self evaluation schemes have overtones of account-ability, their raison d'être is to provide information for school development purposes. Viviane Robinson (in section three) describes the New Zealand experience with school based review: and in a recent report for the OECD, I reviewed twenty-eight different projects in twelve member countries (Hopkins 1983).

The discussion in the previous paragraph indicates the breadth of contemporary school improvement activities, and the degree to which they have increased during the past few years. This trend is confirmed in the OECD School Improvement Project ISIP which was initiated in May 1982 and will run for three years. Much of the preliminary conceptual work for this project was done by Ray Bolam and published by the OECD in 1982. Bolam's revised re-port was called *Strategies for School Improvement*, and in it he takes the concept of the 'problem solving school' as being the major objective for school improvement efforts. He reviews a number of internal school factors that can contribute to this goal: for example, the role of principal, school self-evaluation, teacher self-evaluation, school focused in-service, school based curriculum development, the school's organizational features, and external, support structures at the national and local levels. He also reviews the recent research on educational change for clues for effective innovation strategies. The six themes selected for ISIP by the planning group reflect Bolam's work:

1   school-based review for school improvement
2   principals and internal change agents in the school improve-ment process
3   the role of the external support in school improvement
4   research and evaluation in school improvement
5   school improvement policy
6   conceptual mapping of school improvement

Van Velzen (1982) has outlined these themes in detail, and described the rationale for the project like this:

> The basic rationale for a project on School Improvement is that many OECD member countries are searching for answers to similar issues and that they can learn from each other in using international cooperation to increase their knowledge in the field of school improvement. A combined

effort at international level can also mean a division of labour between countries/institutions to concentrate on different and new issues.

In these last few paragraphs I have illustrated the scope of, and increased emphasis on school improvement in the past two or three years. The main features of the landscape of school improvement are now well defined: the school is widely regarded as the prime unit of change, its autonomy (and that of its constituent members) has become a major goal, and internal and external support systems have been created to achieve this end. Change strategies are increasingly being based on a multi-dimensional concept of implementation tied to the organizational features of the school, and individual school improvement efforts, for example, staff development, or school based curriculum development, are typically conceived of in a wider context. It is interesting to reflect on how quickly the concept has been assimilated into the culture and vernacular of educational change, and how secure the boundaries of its territory have become.

## References

AOKI, T. (1979) *Toward Curriculum Inquiry in a New Key* Occasional Paper No. 2, Edmonton, Department of Secondary Education, University of Alberta.

BERMAN, P. and McLAUGHLIN, M.W. (1977) *Federal Programs Supporting Educational Change. Vol VII* Santa Monica, California, Rand Corporation.

BOLAM, R. (1982) *Strategies for School Improvement* Paris, OECD.

BRITISH COLUMBIA MINISTRY OF EDUCATION. (1979). *Curriculum Planning* Victoria, BC.

DAVID, J.L. (1982) *School Based Strategies: Implications for Government Policy* Bay Area Research Group Mimeo.

EMRICK, J.A. and PETERSON, S.M. (1978) *A Synthesis of Findings Across Five Recent Studies in Educational Dissemination and Change* (Revised). San Francisco, Far West Lab.

FULLAN, M. (1982) *The Meaning of Educational Change* Toronto, OISE Press.

FULLAN, M. and POMFRET, A. (1977) 'Research on curriculum and instruction implementation?' *Review of Educational Research* 47 (1), pp. 335–97.

HABERMAS, J. (1972) *Knowledge and Human Interests* Boston, Beacon Park.

HOPKINS, D. (1983) *School Based Review for School Improvement* Paris, OECD.

ILLICH, I. (1971) *Deschooling Society* Harmondsworth, Penguin.

JOYCE B.R. (1978) *Involvement: A Study of Shared Governance of Teacher Education* Syracuse, National Dissemination Center.

LEHMING, R. and KANE, M. (Eds) *Improving Schools* Beverly Hills, California, Sage.

NISBET, J. (Ed) (1973) *Creativity of the School* Paris, OECD.

RUNKEL, P., SCHMUCK, R., ARENDS, J. and FRANCISCO, R. (1979). *Transforming the Schools Capacity for Problem Solving* Eugene, Oregon, CEPM.

SCHMUCK, R.A. (1973) *Interventions for Strengthening the Schools Creativity* in NISBET (op. cit).

SCHMUCK, R.A. and MILES, M.B. (Eds) (1971) *Organization Development in Schools*, La Jülla, California, University Associates.

STENHOUSE, L. (1975) *An Introduction to Curriculum Research and Development* London, Heinemann.

VAN VELZEN, W. (1979) *Autonomy of the School*, S'Hertogenbosch, Netherlands, KPC.

VAN VELZEN, W. (1982) *Conceptual Mapping of Schooling Improvement* Paris, OECD.

# Characteristics of the Autonomous School

Richard A. Schmuck
University of Oregon

To the casual and unsophisticated observer, schools are simply places in which teachers teach and students learn. Distinctions between different schools are not considered and often not even noticed. But to the people who work and play within the schools – the students, teachers, administrators, and concerned parents – schools are different from one another. Indeed, a school can be said to have its own vibrations and soul; different schools express tones of feeling that are both important and distinguishable from one another. These vibrations come from the interpersonal relationships in the school; they compose the school's 'climate'. Evidence of the school's climate can be seen in how learning activities are carried out, how play occurs, and how school participants typically interact with one another. The term climate is meant to capture the overriding social-emotional tone of the school. As such it has been difficult to study scientifically and as a result, its very importance has been strongly doubted by the academic research community.

## The Legacy of Doubt by Researchers

Even though school participants do experience marked differences in the climate of their schools, a number of significant and widely publicized research reports produced during the past fifteen years have left a 'legacy of doubt' about the importance of school climate. However, prior to the research of Coleman (1966), Plowden (1967), and Jencks *et al* (1972) – not to speak of the significant work of Arthur Jensen (1969) – few researchers in education expressed doubt about whether differences among schools were significant factors in explaining differences in student learning. Indeed, many of the reform movements in education during the fifties and early sixties were built upon the assumption that the 'form' of school organization as well as its climate were significantly related to learning outcomes. Thus, for example, Conant advocated the comprehensive high school, the federal government spent abundant funds to 'equalize' the financial support of schools, and local schools tried a variety of organizational innovations, such as team teaching, differentiated staffing, the open classroom, the open corridor, and the like. In all of these instances, decisions to innovate in the social structure of the school were based not so much on empirical evidence as on an *a priori* acceptance of the tenability of the assumption that differences in schools do make a difference for pupil learning and achievement.

Then came the reports from Coleman, Plowden, and Jencks *et al.*, accompanied also by the Ford Foundation's admissions of failure after a decade of school innovation in Paul Nactigal's (1972) *Ford Goes to School*. All of these carried a message of doubt about the ability of the school – however organized and with whatever climate – to make a difference in student learning.

During the early sixties Coleman conducted a large-scale survey of the achievement of over 600,000 students in 4,000 schools. The results were believed to indicate that educational attainment was largely independent of the school experiences that a pupil underwent. The Coleman report was viewed as a very credible document. It carried considerable weight among policymakers. The data reported in it were reliable and valid, and the analyses were carefully performed. Indeed, one conclusion that low achievers possess a deep sense of powerlessness in relation to schooling has been often cited and several times replicated. Nevertheless, some social psychologists, including myself, questioned the appropriateness of the limited range of variables that Coleman selected to evaluate schools and pupils. Notably missing were variables that described differences in school policies, structures, norms, procedures, affective environments, and level of program implementation. Still, the Coleman report carried weight and it was in line with parallel research that was being done in England.

One year after Coleman, in England, the widely read Plowden Report (1967) was published. It concluded that home influences far outweigh school variables in relation to student achievement. And, while it too suffered from limitations similar to the Coleman study, the Plowden Report took on extra weight because of its similarity in emphasis. Once more the school's programs, its structures, and its climate were thought to be largely irrelevant to teaching and learning.

Still more of the same occurred in 1972 when Jencks and his colleagues reassessed a large volume of statistical data from a number of investigations. Those analyses led to the startling conclusions that:

> equalizing the quality of high schools would reduce cognitive inequality by one percent or less, [and that] additional school expenditures are unlikely to increase achievement and redistribution resources will not reduce test-score inequality.

When the social scientists were asked to account for differences in student outcomes, they answered in very different ways but few saw the school's climate as being relevant. Jensen, of course, firmly proposed heredity. Coleman and Plowden turned to the family. Jencks wrote about plain luck. None placed the school even in second place. Bowles and Gintis (1976) in their Marxist critique of schooling scoffed at eugenics, family dynamics, and luck, proposing that educational inequalities are rooted in basic class subcultures and social biases of our economy. They described how the values of societal subcultures can be learned by students in their interactions with teachers, administrators, and schoolmates, thus coming close to proposing that the school itself could make a difference in student outcomes. Still, they did not directly study linkages between school dynamics and student performances.

## The Glimmer of Light of Researchers

Now, after more than a decade of doubt about the importance of the quality of life in the school for the achievement of students, we have our first, large-scale empirical study to support the hypothesis that school climate can make a difference. It is the work entitled *Fifteen Thousand Hours* by Rutter, Maughan, Mortimore and Ouston (1979). The title is the author's estimate of the amount of time that a typical student spends in the classroom from kindergarten to the end of secondary school. Working out of the Institute of Psychiatry in London, Rutter and his colleagues intensively studied twelve secondary schools in London for three years. The students of those inner-city schools tended by and large to be below the national average in achievement. The schools were all comprehensive, fairly formal, not alternative educational settings. The teachers typically had five to ten years experience and the students were grouped in sets or streams. The schools were not special – they were typical big city, comprehensive high schools in England.

*Richard Schmuck*

The principal concern in the longitudinal research design was to investigate differences between schools in terms of various measures of pupil behavior and attainment, and to determine in what ways the processes of the schools might influence those pupil outcomes. Necessarily, the design included: first, measures of the individual pupils as they entered the school; second, measures of the social processes within the school itself; third, an evaluation of the ways in which pupil outcomes were affected by school processes, after taking into account the effects of individual intake characteristics; and fourth, measures of particular ecological influences to determine whether they were associated with variations in pupil outcome, or with variations in school processes. The team's research methods included direct observations, interviews with staff and pupils, ability and achievement measures and the like.

A thorough summary and critique of this rich and variegated study has been published elsewhere (Exeter University, 1979). And it should certainly be noted that the study's methodology has been strongly criticized by some statisticians (not more so, however, than the large-scale statistical manipulations by Coleman, in Plowden, and by Jencks *et al*). For our purposes here, let us take note of those school processes suggested in the research that may shed light on how climate influences student performance:

1  It is important to note first that the researchers did find marked and distinct differences between schools – that is between the schools' norms, structures, and procedures. The words used in the study are the schools' 'overall style, approach, aims, and ethos'. We might use the word climate to summarize what is meant here.

2  There were large differences between the schools with respect to levels of attendance, pupils' behaviour in school, delinquency, and academic attainment – differences which still remained after controlling for the relevant neighbourhood and student intake variables. While it is true that some of the authors' statistical manipulations should be questioned, it also is apparent just from casual inspection of the numbers and of the school descriptions that significant differences among schools do exist.

3  Physical and administrative arrangements of the schools were not associated with school processes or pupil outcomes.

4  Analyses of ecological influences indicated that, although the

home might have played a small part in influencing their behavior and attainments, those effects did not account for school differences in pupil outcome.

5   Variations between schools in different forms of outcome for their pupils were reasonably stable over periods of at least three years.

6   In general, schools performed fairly similarly on all the various measures of outcome. That is, schools which did better than average in pupils' behaviour in school tended also to do better in terms of exam success and delinquency.

7   The differences among the schools in outcomes were systematically related to their characteristics as human social systems. Factors as varied as the degree of academic emphasis by the staff, teacher actions in the classroom lessons, the incentives and rewards, supportive interpersonal conditions for pupils, and the extent to which pupils were able to take on responsibility were all significantly associated with outcome differences between schools. And it is important to note that according to the statistics made available by the authors, each of the variables in the human social system of the school was open to modification by the staff through concerted action.

With such empirical support in the contemporary literature, concern about the characteristics of the school as an organization can again take on legitimacy as a topic of significance of student development. Now let us set aside, however, the concern in linking school processes with pupil learning, and turn to the major topic of this chapter, those school organizational processes themselves. We will refer to the ideal school climate as the 'Autonomous School'.

## The Autonomous School as an Ideal

It is important to keep in mind that the Autonomous School represents an ideal construct – much in the way sociologists such as Weber, Tonnies, and Park attempted to develop ideal types in their analyses of organizations, communities, and societies. As such, the Autonomous School is based only partially on the empirical data of our experiences and of the sort of research that *15,000 Hours* offers. We must add to our observations of actual schools a considerable amount of imagination to establish a vision of the Autonomous School. It is, in other words, an ideal construct that offers a target toward which we would try to gear school improvement efforts.

Thus, the concept of the Autonomous School as an ideal construct offers a scale against which we can assess where any school might be, in what ways that school should change, and how far it must go to obtain the ideal state. There will obviously be many different visions of the ideal, and ultimately correct answers must be derived empirically by returning to studies to test linkages between school processes and student learning. For now, there are a few glimpses of some characteristics of the Autonomous School that seem appropriate.

## The Dutch Conference

First, let us draw on some ideas from a conference held in 1979 in the Netherlands for the purpose of guiding school improvement during the next decade in that country. Three ideal types of schools were contrasted at that conference; for more details see VanVelzen (1979).

Initially, schools in which autonomous teachers are the dominant factor were discussed. We can refer to such a school as having a highly individuated structure for instruction. In such schools, teachers hold primary responsibility for providing instruction in a particular classroom or in a particular subject. Teachers are free in the planning of classes and in the teaching itself. Teachers were not obliged typically to take on activities outside teaching hours. Consultation between teachers is highly sporadic. Indeed, it is mainly concerned with entry of new students, allowing students to pass from one class to the next, or when rather serious crises occur in the school.

The second type of school is one in which the division of responsibilities is hierarchical. The centre of authority in this type of school can lie either with school management or with the appropriate (public) authorities. In such schools teachers are typically not autonomous in their teaching. School management may make decisions concerning the content of education and instruct teachers to put those decisions into effect, if necessary in cooperation with one another.

The third type, the Autonomous School, is a school in which value emphasis is placed on cooperation between different levels. Responsibilities are shared between the school management, the teachers, the non-teaching staff, the parents, and the students.

Compared with the first school type, the teachers of the Autonomous School have a more limited autonomy in their teaching, while compared to the second type, the teachers of the Autonomous School have much more to say about the school's operation and procedures. Typically, teachers in the Autonomous School basically perform a triad of tasks. They are:

1　to teach in a particular organization context;
2　to take part in the work of a subject group – a team, or a departmental unit;
3　to carry out a number of duties in the school decided through staff deliberations.

## The Lewin, Lippitt, and White Research

In reflecting on the Autonomous School, as it was portrayed at the Dutch Conference, one is struck by the similarity between this typology of organizations and the typology of leadership styles that was created by Lewin, Lippitt, and White in their classical studies of the late 1930s. The three leadership styles were autocratic, democratic, and *laissez-faire*. For more details, see White and Lippitt (1960).

The dynamics of the school in which the autonomous teacher is a dominant factor are similar to the social processes associated with *laissez-faire* leadership. The *laissez-faire* school principal, for example, would exert influence only very rarely, allowing staff members to do mostly as they wish. Of course, while the teachers under such leadership are free to perform their classroom roles as they wish, there is at the same time a low amount of group energy, interpersonal collaboration and staff cohesiveness. In this connection Lewin's research showed that when the members of *laissez-faire* led groups attempted to work together, they experienced frustration, disorgnization and low productivity, becoming convinced through their ineffectiveness that the best way to solve problems was to allow every member to execute problem solving on his or her own. A similar set of circumstances would no doubt often occur in schools featured by the autonomous teacher.

In a definite contrast to the permissiveness of the *laissez-faire* leader, the school in which the division of responsibilities is hierarchical calls for an authoritarian style of leadership. In schools of a hierarchical sort, power resides in the legitimate position of the principal and influence is delegated primarily to subheads who are duly designated as representatives of the principal. Lewin's research indicated that while groups with authoritarian leaders tended to produce well in the short run and especially under pressure, they also were characterized by competitiveness, underlying hostility, and high dependency. Indeed the emotional interference that arises under authoritarian regimes typically reduces satisfaction and productivity in the long run.

During the past decade, a considerable number of efforts to engineer school change in the United States have been accompanied by increasing authoritarian and hierarchical pressures. The top-down strategy for school improvement is taken as an antidote to the disorganization and permissiveness inspired by the *laissez-faire*, autonomous secondary school. Through increased formal structure, social pressure, expert direction, and supervisory monitoring, it is believed by advocates of hierarchical change that autonomous teachers can be coerced to conform to a new set of instructional procedures and working relationships with colleagues. The hierarchical strategies of the past decade in secondary schools have been in the form of urging teachers to write behavioral objectives, convincing instructional departments to use program planning and budgeting systems, increasing the number of high status teachers in district-wide instructional task forces, bringing in curriculum experts to tell teachers how to teach differently, introducing behaviour modification tactics for classroom management, and increasing the amount of supervision, observation, and monitoring of everyone including principals, teachers, and students. It frequently occurs, of course, that once the pressures of hierarchy are removed, compliant principals, teachers, and students return to their preferred ways of doing things, again hiding within the norm of autonomy.

## The OECD Conference

Another way of approaching the ideal concept of the Autonomous School was developed at a conference sponsored by the Organization of Economic Cooperation and Development (OECD) in 1972. The results of that meeting have been published in a monograph by Van Gendt (1974). Interestingly, while that conference predated the now widely-read Rand study by Berman and McLaughlin (1975–78), many of the concepts of the two are overlapping and mutually supported. The core idea is that a productive school has the capabilites of being creative as a collective entity. Thus, through collaboration, interdependence, and joint problem solving, the staff members of a school can take proper initiative in responding to innovations and new circumstances impinging on the school from the outside. The creative school is one in which the faculty and the student body, working in close harmony, can both adopt new ideas so that they are maximally useful to the school, and reject those innovations that do not fit into the school's scheme or plan. That idea of the creatively collaborative and initiating school served as a foundation to some of the subsequent conceptualizing about the 'Autonomous School' that occurred at Oregon during the seventies.

## The R and D Program at Oregon

For more than a decade, Philip Runkel and I, along with perhaps a hundred collaborators, have been attempting to create a conceptual scheme to describe the 'Autonomous School'. We refer to the object of our inquiry as the 'school's capacity for problem solving'. Our experiences in several large urban school districts and in eight different interventions in organization development have led us to conceive of a school's problem-solving capacity in ways very similar to those generated by the Dutch, in OECD, and by the studies on innovation by Rand. The results of our efforts were published a few years ago (see Runkel, Schmuck, Arends, and Francisco, 1979, for details).

To summarize briefly, we view the capacity for problem solving in a school to be constituted of four meta-skills that are institutionalized. The first – that of systematic diagnosis – is the staff's ability to assess the current functioning of the school. This would involve collecting data to ascertain current states of affairs and collecting data to evaluate change efforts, new programs, and the like. The second – that of searching for information and resources – is the staff's ability to initiate and execute searches inside or outside the school for information and resources that are relevant to the diagnosed problems. The third – that of mobilizing collaborative action – is the staff's ability to form quickly into *ad hoc* groups or the staff as a whole to carry out problem solving or to actualize the information that has been brought into the school to solve an assessed problem. This third skill also involves what psychologists refer to as 'synergy' – achieving through a group more than what could be achieved by the members working separately or in parallel. The fourth – that of monitoring – is the staff's ability to evaluate how effectively the first three meta-skills are being carried out and to put into play remedial actions that will repair weaknesses.

To achieve this enhanced capacity for problem solving, certain norms, roles, and patterns of communication and influence would be necessary. The Autonomous School would be characterized by norms that support collaboration and confrontation, the rights and integrity of all, the cognitive and affective growth of all, and the freedom of participants to pursue own goals. Other norms would encourage the behaviour of: direct, open and authentic communication; creative risk-taking to find new ways to solve problems; public discussion on the dynamics of the group itself; and critical assessment of school operations by both staff and students. It would house organizational roles that are: defined clearly so that participants know what others expect of them; flexible so that participants' functions are consonant with their interests and capabilities rather than only their status; changeable so that students may teach, teachers may learn, and all are seen as potentially helpful to one another. It would have communication that is free-flowing across status positions, personal and direct, and skilful, utilizing learned procedures of listening, paraphrasing, etc. Finally, the Autonomous School would have power and influence that is clearly defined, shared, and dispersed so that all persons perceive that they can have some impact upon the affairs of the school.

I would like also to put considerable emphasis on the quality of life for the students. I believe that the Autonomous School is more likely to become a reality to the extent that we are capable of imagining a cooperative school culture that includes the students as an integral part. I see the Autonomous School as working better if the cooperative spirit fully engages the student body as well as the teachers and administrators. Moreover, the school's viability will be strengthened to the degree that students collaborate with teachers in solving educational and organizational problems. In other words the Autonomous School puts emphasis on cooperation between the various levels, including relationships between students and educators as well as students with one another, such that the students will feel more involved and committed to working with others to make the school experience both academically and personally fulfilling.

## Summary

In this chapter, an attempt has been made to present the case for the importance of the ideal construct of the Autonomous School. The point of departure for this case is the assumption that all school improvement efforts need targets toward which they are moving. And by counterposing the recent English Study, *Fifteen Thousand Hours*, against the 'legacy of doubt' engendered by the writings of Coleman, Plowden, and Jencks, I have sought to lend credibility to a focus on the school organization as the target for improvement.

Several international conferences and publications, along with the results of our own R and D work at Oregon, serve as the foundation upon which a description of the characteristics of the Autonomous are posed. Some of the key characteristics are productive interdependence among teachers and students, self-analytic diagnoses of the school's performance by the staff, a proactive reaching out for information and resources, an ability to bring staff and students together for problem solving, and a continuous self-reflective monitoring of all of the above. The Autonomous School possesses a supportive, affective climate in which the educators and the students work together to adopt or to reject educational innovations. As such, the Autonomous School can be said to be creative as a social system and to possess the capacity to solve its own problems.

## References

BERMAN, P. and McLAUGHLIN, M.W. (1975–1978) *Federal Programs Supporting Educational Change, Vol. I-VIII* Santa Monica, California, Rand Corporation

BOWLES, S. and GINTIS, H. (1976) *Schooling in Capitalist America* New York, Basic Books.

COLEMAN, J. (1966) *Equality in Educational Opportunity* Washington, U.S. Government Printing Office.

EXETER UNIVERSITY. (1979) *The Rutter Research: Perspectives I* Exeter, School of Education.

JENCKS, C., SMITH, M., ACLAND, H., BANE, M.J., COHEN, D.K., GINTIS, H., HENYNS, B. and MICHELSON, S. (1972) *Inequality* New York, Basic Books.

JENSEN, A.R. (1969) 'How much can we boost IQ and scholastic achievement?' *Harvard Educational Review*, 39, 1–123.

NACTIGAL, P. (1972) *Ford Goes to School* New York, Ford Foundation.

PLOWDEN REPORT. (1967) *Children and Their Primary Schools* London, HMSO.

*Richard Schmuck*

RUNKEL, P., SCHMUCK, R., ARENDS, J. and FRANCISCO, R. (1979) *Transforming the School's Capacity for Problem-Solving* Eugene, Oregon, CEPM.

RUTTER, M., MAUGHAN, B., MORTIMORE, P., and OUSTON, J. (1979) *Fifteen Thousand Hours* London, Open Books Publishing Limited.

VAN GENDT, R. (Ed) (1974) *Creativity of the School* Paris, OECD.

VAN VELZEN, W. (Ed) (1979) *Autonomy of the School* S'Hertogenbusch, Netherlands, KPC.

WHITE, R. and LIPPITT, R. (1960) *Autocracy and Democracy* New York, Harper Brothers.

# Improvement or Not – That is the Question?

Mats Ekholm
School Leader Education in Sweden

## Introduction

Young people of today know a great deal more than young people did yesterday. Many facts and ideas that are fully alive in the mind of a fifteen year old nowadays, were never dreamt about by their grandparents. The young people of today are exposed to a wider 'knowledge market' than was common in former years. The group of information about international events is an example where information about what is happening comes directly through the modern mass media. However, as young people have been brought up to adjust to the media's way to inform, they seem to have lost some of the talent to become informed about their own close environment and how to cope with it.

In the process of learning during the first twenty years of life, school is an important component. Through the work in school, we expect the young to become familiar with the use of the tools of our culture which will enable them to conserve and to develop that culture. There have always been discussions about the way in which schools fulfil this function. There seems to have been no period during which people have been totally happy with their schools. There is always a need for schools to improve. In my home country, Sweden, we have been occupied with attempts to improve our schools since they were established.

The school improvement efforts have varied historically. In the early years of this century, we were occupied with changes in the curriculum so that the educational process could be developed on the basis of the child, instead of adults. Also, we tried to improve our schools by changing the curriculum. For example, in Sweden, the time that was spent on religious education was reduced to accommodate other subjects. Later in the century we sought to improve Swedish schools by keeping our young people together for their first nine school years in the same school. This practice is still not common in the European scene where the selection of the students starts much earlier than in Northern America.

During these periods, as now, there have been lively debates as to whether schools were really providing the young with a good education. In the forties there were voices raised (Arvidsson, 1948) that the youth were badly educated to write and to read. Similar voices have been heard during the later part of the seventies. The critics now say that the youth of today have received an education given without demands from teachers. The critics in Sweden have cried for the same things that have been heard from almost all Western countries – back to basics. And they have combined their cries with demands for more ordered working patterns in schools that seem to be copies of what teachers used when the critics themselves went to school – more repetition, less freedom for the young, more power to the teachers, more direct teaching and less exploratory education.

Sweden is a small nation with not more than eight million inhabitants. Approximately one million attend schools and some one hundred thousand work as teachers. Therefore the school improvement attempts that I have just described have involved the entire nation. Improvement from one point of view is not necessarily seen as improvement from other points of view. The curriculum changes that took place in the early twenties, in which the religious part of the total curriculum was given less time and in which the language training was based more on the logic of the child than on the logic of the grammar, were from the viewpoints of religious people and from the viewpoints of some linguists of that time, real disasters. The debate about the good and bad in the creation of a comprehensive school that passed the parliament in 1949 still continues. Those who have political views that favour equality and cooperation find this innovation to be a real improvement. Those who have political standpoints that put stronger emphasis on competition and are not so much in favour of the philosophy of equality, do not find these innovations to be an improvement. It is not a research question to judge if a change process is an improvement. It is a political question. Therefore, when we are discussing school improvement, we must keep the value questions in mind. It seems necessary to demand from those who present studies about school improvement to be explicit about the value context in which such attempts have been conducted.

## Some Limitations of the Existing Research

Many of the studies dealing with school improvement in Western countries involve schools that have extra resources for the improvement process. It is also common that the researcher has some kind of linkage to the methods used to get the school to function better (that is, Baker, 1980; Schmuck *et al*, 1975; Pratt, Thurber and Hall, 1982). Such studies aim at comparisons between those situations intended to improve schools and the *status quo*. Thus, in the growth of the knowledge base about the school improvement process, it seems to me that we lack studies aimed at seeing what occurs in schools where no outside explicit attempts at change are involved. In particular, there seems to be a need for studies of the natural change process that might take place in schools having no enthusiastic project leader or change agent available. Keith and Smith (1971), Gross *et al* (1971) and Miles (1978) have presented studies that are in line with what I believe we need to be able to understand the more common process of school improvement.

Studies of school improvements typically deal with a very limited time perspective. It is exceptional to find a study which has collected data about changes occurring two or three years after the change process has been started. The rule is to collect data very close to the end of the period of the 'attempted implementation of an organizational innovation' to borrow a term from Gross *et al* (1971). This means that data are collected within a year or two after the change attempt was started. This is done by researchers who seem to be very much aware of the fact that a change in a social organization takes much longer time than just a couple of years.

Thus, research must seek to understand the long term change process in those schools where no special help from talented change agents have occurred. In the section that follows, I present results from two studies in which it is possible to illuminate the natural change process, that sometimes is an improvement and sometimes not, in selected Swedish comprehensive schools.

## Two Swedish Studies

In the first of these studies, I compared school climates as they were perceived by students and staff in twelve comprehensive schools at two points in time, 1969 and 1979, Grade eight (fifteen year old) students and their teachers were administered the same questionnaire in 1979 that had been given 10 years earlier. [The number of students that answered the questionnaire were 1590 in 1969 and 1501 in 1979. Ninety percent of all the students who belonged to the eighth grade in the twelve schools answered the questionnaire. Those who did not respond were absent from school on the day that the questionnaire was administered due to normal reasons such as illness etc. The teachers received the questionnaire by mail and their response rate is much lower than the response rate for the students – 72% in 1969 and 57% in 1979.] The twelve schools, which represented three different kinds of municipalities in the Western part of Sweden, collectively provide a reflection of ten years of struggle for better schooling.

In order to present and interpret some of the rich data resulting from the ten-year comparison I first explain some basic facts about the Swedish system for the in-service training of teachers.

## In-service Training in Swedish Schools

As mentioned earlier, the Swedish schools have a strong tradition, exercised over many years, of improving themselves. The geographic shape of the country and the dispersed population have brought teachers together since the beginning of the century to meet with colleagues and to engage in educational discussions. As early as the thirties teachers in individual schools held what was called pedagogical days when children were free from school. When the Swedish school system was transformed to the comprehensive school system in the early sixties, study days for the teachers were institutionalized in the Swedish schools. During these five study days all teachers within a principal's area (two or three schools under one principal's administration) met to discuss educational developments of a general nature or to discuss how to handle local problems in the specific schools that belong to the principal's area. The main purpose of these study days were to improve the work in the schools.

Between the years 1969 and 1979, the total number of study days in each of the twelve schools that participated in the ten-year study would have totalled fifty. Ten to fifteen of these study days were used by the schools for local planning, and during the other days there would have been in-service training programmes. The content of this training did not involve a specific plan which is typical of Swedish schools. Most schools in Sweden do not create a long term plan for the in-service training of their teachers. The program during the study days are planned from year to year built on a mixture of central intentions and local needs. That means that the thirty-five to forty in-service occasions that each school had during the ten years have been used for a wide range of activities. Time has been spent on co-operation training, group dynamics, new developments within teaching subjects, problem analysis within the school, discussions about the new central curriculum and alternative working methods to be used in the classroom among other topics. [In Sweden all comprehensive schools are following the same guidelines, that are presented in what is called 'Laroplan for Grundskolan' (Central Curriculum for the Comprehensive School). This central curriculum is given to the schools by the government after being heard in parliament.]

### Working Methods – The Development Over Ten Years

One of the consistent improvements that the Swedish society has striven for during this ten year period has been to make the day to day work in the classroom more varied. Through many channels the message has been clear – less direct teaching (traditional teacher talk and questioning with students responding) and more of the exploratory working methods with a higher degree of student involvement. The message was presented in the central curriculum, through journals of the teacher unions and it was brought out during study days and also during summer courses in which some of the teachers of the twelve schools participated. A measurement of the effect of this improvement attempt is presented in table 1.

Table 1 is based on answers from students and teachers to the questions: 'You have many different subjects and teachers in school. The class works in many different ways. How often are the working methods presented below used in your class?' (Students); and 'How frequently do you use the following working methods in your daily teaching?' (Teachers). Both teachers and students were presented with descriptions of five working methods and were asked to mark if the five specific methods were used several times per day, once a day, once a week, sometimes during a month, almost never or never. In table 1 frequencies for those students and teachers in all the twelve schools are shown that have given the answers 'several times per day' or 'once a day'.

The results that are presented in table 1 give a rather evident picture of what happened over the ten years – very little changed. Both teachers and students judge the daily use of the five different working methods in the same way in 1969 and in 1979. There are only

*Table 1  Percentage of Students and Teachers in Twelve Swedish Comprehensive Schools who Reported on the Daily Occurrence of Teaching Practices in 1969 and 1979.*

| Students | 1969 % | 1979 % | Teachers | 1969 % | 1979 % |
|---|---|---|---|---|---|
| 1 The class listens and the teacher talks | 81 | 81 | 1 You lecture the subject while the students listen | 36 | 46 |
| 2 The teacher talks and puts questions. Single students answer the questions | 85 | 77 | 2 You lecture the subject, put questions on it and the students answer and listen | 67 | 67 |
| 3 The teacher and the class discuss together | 19 | 24 | 3 You and the class discuss the subject and related questions together | 58 | 64 |
| 4 Group work with specific tasks | 2 | 4 | 4 The students work in groups with specific tasks and you are available to them | 30 | 43 |
| 5 The students work one by one with individual tasks | 38 | 48 | 5 The students work individually with specific tasks. You are available to them | 56 | 63 |

small shifts in some of the perceptions for both teachers and students.

Teachers as well as students on both occasions found that the traditional methods (1 and 2) were used frequently every day. There are more students than teachers, reporting that this is the case, both in the case of the pure lecture and the question-answer kind of lesson.

There are several possible interpretations of this difference. The teachers were more aware of what was intended, and they occupied different social positions than the students in school. Perhaps the most striking interpretation of the differences between the students' and their teachers' perception of what is going on in the classroom is that the teachers' judgement is strongly influenced by their ideal views of the working process. They report more frequently what *ought* to have happened instead of what *did* happen. The students are in their testimonies free from this kind of bias – they have very little knowledge of the ideals for the working process and therefore report a more factual situation.

However, my focus in this chapter is not on how teachers and students view the work in the classroom, but rather the changes that have occurred over the ten year period. Both students and teachers report a greater daily emphasis on discussion (item 3) and individual work (item 5) in 1979 than was reported in 1969. A greater percentage of teachers in 1979 reported spending more time daily on group work (item 4) than they did in 1969, but a similar shift was also evident in the case of lecturing (item 1). However, when one examines the student data, the shift from lecturing to group work over the ten year period, the change is really not that evident.

Direct observations of the use of working methods in Swedish schools that we conducted in the middle of the seventies (Ekholm, 1976), where fifty-four classes were observed during three days, justifies the testimonies from the students. I then described what was going on in the ordinary classroom in the following way (Ekholm, 1976:11):

> The school work pattern showed itself to be relatively monotonous. Observation results show that pupils worked mainly by themselves on an identical task. Besides this work method, the hours in class were dominated by the teacher speaking, in the form of explaining the subject and then asking questions. Pupils seldom did any form of collective work other than being together in the same room. Classroom work was steered mainly by the subject taught and the textbook and/or teaching materials, and to a certain degree by the teacher.

When we look at the differences over the ten years with the students' results in focus, we can conclude that the working pattern in the school is very stable. There was a small tendency for students and teachers to report more discussion in 1979 than in 1969 and it was more common in 1979 than in 1969 that the students worked on individual tasks. When we look at the teachers' perspective we can note that there are more teachers in 1979 who say that they use lectures, discussions, group work as well as individual tasks in their day to day work in the schools. The conclusion for the total picture is that the teachers during the ten year period have become more aware of the demands for more varied working patterns in the school. Their willingness to use group work and discussions, during which the students can be more active, have grown through the years, which also is to be seen as an improvement when compared to the values that the Swedish system is based on. The schools seem to have improved with regard to the attitudes of the teachers. The study days seem to have had some of the effects they were expected to have. But in such a relatively short period of time, that ten years when we studied social changes, the working habits and routines seem not to have changed in the same way that the attitudes of the teachers have changed. Certainly, the changes have not been such that the students are perceiving the daily use of working methods in a new way.

One of the teaching approaches that did provide a shift over the ten year period according to both teachers and students was the individual work of students (item 5). What are the roots of this change? One explanation can be found in the teachers' participation in study days and their absorption of the messages from the society about specified changes of the school life. However, this change may have been a mechanized, technical change rather than one grounded in the in-service training of teachers. The reality behind this change in working method seems to be linked to ready made teaching aids in the form of work books and teachers mimeos. During the ten years that have passed between the two survey occasions, the development of copying machines has been very rapid. By the help of these machines and by the growing market of pre-produced working materials, greater possibilities for the teachers to engage students in individual work has occurred. But most students are working with the same tasks at the same time. The reason for the shift in the use of this working method seems to be a rather materialistic one, which gives the teacher a better work economy and at the same time leads to a more mechanical way of working in the schools. This shift doesn't seem to be an adjustment to the developmental level of the student. It is not a question of a larger individualization of the school work. It seems to be a more effective way to direct the work of the student.

So far I have shown the overall picture of the changes over the ten years. But what about the single school? Is there the same development in all of the schools studied? In figures 1 and 2 the results are shown for each of the twelve schools on two of the working methods – the individual work and the discussions between teachers and students.

If we use the views of the students as our main source of data about individual students work in the classroom, there seems to have been a general change over all schools (Figure 1). However, when we consider the situation from the teachers' point of view, the general pattern is not so evident. In five of the schools the change is very small or nonexistent. In two of the schools the change is small but opposite to the student pattern. In five of the schools the changes are evident and in the same direction as those of the students. In these five schools we can talk reliably about a change in the way students work individually. That these changes represent an improvement is, however, as I mentioned before, doubtful.

In figure 2, I have chosen to show, for each of the twelve schools, how many students and teachers who say that there are discussions in class between students and teachers every day. What seemed to be a general pattern in table 1 (where in 1979 both students and teachers

*Figure 1    Percentage of students and teachers who report that students work individually with specific tasks every day.*

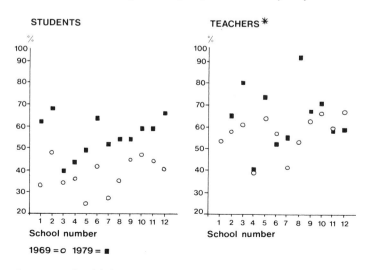

STUDENTS     TEACHERS *

1969 = o   1979 = ■

* School 1 got such a high no-answer rate among the teachers that it is not presented here

*Mats Ekholm*

*Figure 2   Percentage of students and teachers who say that the teacher and the class discuss together every day.*

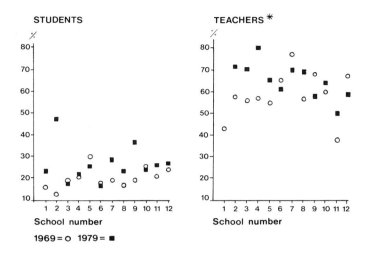

STUDENTS          TEACHERS *

School number          School number

1969 = o   1979 = ■

* School 1 got such a high no-answer rate among the teachers that it is not presented here

more frequently say that the teacher and the class discuss each day) is not a general pattern in this case. In four of the schools (schools 2, 7, 8 and 11) both students and teachers have more frequently in 1979 than in 1969 said that there are daily discussions between the teacher and the class. In these schools there seems to have been an improvement of the working methods; in the other schools, there are no signs of this improvement.

## Changes in Work Load

Another question in the study dealt with the work load of the students. Students were asked the question 'How often do you usually have homework during an ordinary school week?'. Eighty-seven percent of the boys and 95% of the girls in 1969 said that they had homework to do almost each day or each day in the week. In 1979, 64% of the boys and 74% of the girls said the same thing.

Behind this change in work load of the students lies a plea from the central authorities for a less overloaded working situation for the students in the comprehensive school. In the central curriculum that was presented in 1969 there were recommendations given to the teachers to be more careful with their homework assignments, as studies had shown that the leisure time of the students tended to disappear. The plea for a new homework norm was also spread through journals and through discussions among the teachers. The results of my study show that this campaign seems to have had effect. The work load among the students is lower in 1979 than in the 1969. On another question the students have estimated how much time they work each day in their home with school tasks. In 1979 there were 62% of the boys and 52% of the girls who used *less* than an hour each day to do their homework. In 1969, 49% of the boys and 31% of the girls said that they used less than an hour on their homework.

Is this change in the working habits of the students a change for the better or for worse? Some people find the change to be for the worse as they think that the students learn less when they spend less time on their studies. Others say that it is an improvement that all students are treated alike and given the same chance to learn in an environment where there are professional people available to help them. These different opinions are represented differently in the twelve schools. There are schools in the studied group in which about 90% of the students in 1979 say that they have homework to do every school day, and other schools in which only about 30% say that they have homework to do every day. In 1969 the variations between the schools were much smaller. The lowest proportion of students who then said that they had homework to do each day was around 80% and the highest proportion was 100%.

What happened during the ten year period with the work load of the teachers that participated in the survey? In table 2 the medians of time that the teachers say that they spend on their job outside their regulated work in the classroom is presented.

In Sweden the working time of the teachers is regulated through collective negotiations between the central authorities and the teachers' unions. The work load is defined by the amount of lessons that a teacher has to do each week. An academic teacher working in the comprehensive school has to do twenty-four forty minute lessons per week in the class in his subjects. A teacher who is working with non-academic subjects, (handicrafts or physical education) has to do twenty-nine lessons per week. In table 1, both types of teachers are included. As can be seen in the table the teachers are working less time in 1979 than in 1969. The differences between the two occasions are statistically significant for the male teachers and not significant for the female teachers. The roots of the differences between the sexes reflects the different traditions of work differentiation in Swedish

*Table 2    Median time that teachers in twelve Swedish comprehensive schools work each day, outside their regular lessons.* *

| | Men** | | Women | |
|---|---|---|---|---|
| | *1969* | *1979* | *1969* | *1979* |
| Median time in hours per day outside giving lessons to class | 2 h 20 min | 1 h 48 min | 1 h 49 min | 1 h 36 min |

* Including such activities as contacts with parents, conferences, assessments of written tests etc.

** The differences between the median scores for both men and women were tested using chi square. The chi square for men was 7.74 (P = .01) and for women 1.53 (P = .30).

homes, where women still have more responsiblity than men. This tradition creates a smaller possibility for the female teacher to engage in her work outside classroom activities.

The results from the study show that the teachers have cut down their working time in the same way as the students had. The decreasing working time is a fact in all but two of the twelve schools in the sample. In the traditional debate in Sweden about the work load among teachers, the view that the teachers' working time has grown instead of decreased is strongly put forward by the teachers' unions. They see an increase of the working time as an impairment, so they ought to see a decrease as an improvement. But is this shortening of the teachers' working time an improvement? In what way does the shorter working time affect the quality of the education?

## The Cognitive Learning of the Students

In what way has the students' learning changed during the seventies? Did they learn more or less, better or worse in the late seventies. Unfortunately I have not succeeded in collecting information to illuminate these questions in the ten year study. There are results of knowledge tests available at the first survey occasion, but not at the second. Although this is the situation, it is possible to give some illustrations of what has happened during the ten years in Sweden at large by the use of the results from another study.

Murray (1978) has analyzed the results of the standardization of knowledge tests that were used in Swedish schools during the seventies to control the quality of the knowledge of the students in different stages of the comprehensive school. She has compared the results for nationwide samples of students during the period 1967 to 1978. In her study, Murray shows, that there are no signs of either improvements nor impairments during the studied decade in the results on the knowledge tests among students of the same age as those who participated in my study. If it is possible to draw generalizations from the study Murray has done, and I think it is so as the samples that have been used are representative of the Swedish students, there are probably no changes in the students' learning results over the ten years. This assumption seems reasonable also in the light of the small changes in the use of working methods that have been reported here. The only evident change that seems to have occurred has to do with the time that students spend on homework. The shift I have noted here is, if we look at the total amount of time that the students use for learning, of minor importance. The loss of this learning time may very well have been compensated by more concentrated work during school hours or by the influence of other learning sources than school.

## The Social Learning

However, there are other learning ambitions in Swedish schools besides cognitive ones. In the *School Regulations* (chapter 5, 1) it is stated,

> The school shall, through its atmosphere and environment, develop the pupils' self-reliance and independent judgement, as well as accustom them to honesty, consideration, attentiveness toward others and good manners.

As can be seen in this quotation the Swedish school is also trying to stimulate social development of the students. In the ten year study I have also tried to illuminate what has happened to the efforts of the school to influence this development. One of the questions that was used to measure the degree of independent behaviours among the students was formulated in the following way:

> Imagine that your teacher gives you a task. You are as quick as possible to find out how a certain thing is produced. The teacher has told you how to do it: go to the library and read about it in a book. But you yourself can figure out another

way that is quicker. Perhaps you can get this information from someone you know who works in such production, or by ringing up a factory, or in some other way. Which way do you choose?

1    ( )    Do as your teacher told you, and go to the library.
2    ( )    Ask your teacher if you may do as you yourself have thought of.
3    ( )    Do as you yourself have figured out without first asking the teacher.

Not only the students were asked to answer this question but also their teachers. I asked them to tell how they would like the student to act in the situation that is described in the quoted question. The answers from the teachers are presented in table 3.

The results show that the positive attitude towards the students' independence in the school situation has become somewhat more embraced in the end of the seventies than it was in the end of the sixties. It is an attitudinal development that is more evident among female teachers than among male teachers. In relation to the ambitions of the society the school seems to have improved in this area during the studied decade.

This is true if we stay with the results for the teachers. When we look at the answers from the students, however there are no signs of improvement. Both in 1969 and in 1979 the great majority of the students (seven boys out of ten and eight girls out of ten) declared

*Table 3    Percentage of teachers answering how they would like a student to act when there is a possibility to choose an independent way to solve a school task.*

| I would like the | Men | | Women | |
|---|---|---|---|---|
| student to | *1969* | *1979* | *1969* | *1979* |
| do as I told him and go to the library | 0 | 4 | 6 | 1 |
| go and ask me if he can do as he had thought on his own | 71 | 61 | 76 | 67 |
| do as he thought himself without asking me | 26 | 34 | 14 | 29 |

N   1969 = 269
N   1979 = 201

that they would have asked the teachers permission to do what they had thought of themselves. Only a minor proportion (about one out of ten) said that they would follow their own idea first. The changes in the attitudes among the teachers have left no traces in the attitudes of the students. It seems as if the students have not noticed the changed attitudes among the adults in the schools. The whole system of the school is here something of a hindrance towards a change. The students believe that the teachers have lower expectations of them than they really do in relation to the aims of the social development of the school. In other questions that were used to catch the degree of independence among the students (in which I ask them about their way of acting in less school related situations) the comparisons between 1969 and 1979 show that a lot more students in 1979 act more independently than in 1969. This result suggests to me that other socialization agents, like the family, have been more evident in showing their positive attitudes towards the independent behaviour among youth than the school still is. An improvement of the up-bringing of the youth has occurred in the society, but the improvement is not occurring in the school.

Also other results from the study show that the relation between teachers and students in the Swedish comprehensive school has not improved during the studied decade. The teachers have very high ambitions for the students' way of treating socially deviant students. The results of the study over the ten years show that the students become less tolerant towards socially deviant students (Ekholm, 1982). Analysis of the correlations of the teachers' and the students' answers in the different schools in 1969 showed that there was a positive correlation, which meant that students in schools where teachers held high ambitions for their tolerance towards deviancy also had the most tolerant attitudes. In 1979 this correlation had disappeared, which might mean that the content of the relation between teachers and students in the studied school has become less oriented towards the social development of the students.

## Conclusions and Some Explanations

The most striking result of the ten year study in Sweden is the great stability that has prevailed in the schools. Most changes that have been noted are small and there are many areas that have been studied where no changes at all seem to have occurred. As I argued in the introduction to this chapter one can also doubt if the changes really are to be seen as improvements, which, again, brings the concept of improvement under debate. To be able to talk about improvement you have to rely on some values. In the case of the Swedish schools this is not a difficult task as we base our school work on declared political values that are presented in the school regulations and in the central curriculum of the school. Another goal of the Swedish school is to make its inner life highly democratic. The teachers shall have a lot of influence over their working situation. And so shall the students. The results from the ten year study indicate that the teachers have a great deal of power over the school situation, but leave very little to the students. The situation does not seem to have improved in this area during the seventies for the students. The results of the study also indicate that there is not very much change in the schools, even over a ten year period during which a system of in-service training occurred occupying thirty-five full working days. What accounts for such stability in a system which was given a clear direction for change and a mandate to implement such change? To answer this question, I turn to the results of a four year study of three comprehensive schools in Sweden (Ekholm and Sandstrom, 1983).

Of course there are many possible explanations why so little has changed during the seventies in Swedish schools but I will concentrate on just one.

One researcher in each school spent about 30–40% of his time observing and interviewing. The main purpose of the study was to understand the process of change in the comprehensive schools, which were under pressure from society to change along the lines described earlier. In this study we found the same low degree of change and improvement as I have reported earlier in this chapter. Therefore, we turned our research efforts more and more to explain the phenomena of stability instead of change. One of the explanations that has become very evident to us has to do with the decision making system of the local Swedish school. One of the researchers who has studied a local school for four years writes in his report about the existing decision making system in his school (Sandstrom, 1983, p. 27).

> After a matter has reached the school leader, some of the matters are dealt with immediately by the school leaders in their function as 'gate keepers'. Through this procedure some minor matters are taken care of not to overload the other working routines. The matters that pass through the 'gate keepers' are worked through by committees. At the first

available staff conference (in which all adults in the school participate) the actual matter is transferred to a committee. This committee is composed of people who are judged to be able to deal with the actual matter, but at the same time there is an ambition to spread out committee work to as many as possible of the school members. In the weekly 'school paper' the committee informs about its work. In the 'subject group' meetings, a discussion is held about what the committee has said in the matter as a preparation for the real decision that is taken in the staff conference. During this conference all adults that are working in the school are present. Most decision are made through acclamation. If voting is necessary the principle 'one man – one vote' is used.

He reports that few teachers were aware of this decision making process. The description that the teachers gave of the decision making system in their own school varied to a large extent and many of the teachers were conscious only of minor parts of the whole system.

Sandstrom (1983) finds from his analysis of four years in the same school that these decision making procedures frequently become ends in themselves. Many of the objectives and intended reforms disappear in the process. Many decisions are reached, but never implemented or realised. He also points to the fact that there is a very loose linkage between a decision made at the school and what happens afterwards. Seldom does anyone in the school have the task of controlling or monitoring how the adults follow the guidelines that a specific decision in the staff conference has made. Therefore, many proposals for change and decisions about new ways to solve old problems are not put into practice.

One of the many conclusions that can be drawn from the work reported in this chapter is that if school improvement is to occur there needs to be more factors involved than pressures from the surrounding society and possibilities given to the teachers to be responsible for their own development. It is not enough to give the teachers the opportunity to improve the school they are working in. This work has to be organized and plans have to be made for longer periods than one year. It also seems to be a necessity for outside persons to be involved in the school to help the teachers diagnose the situation in the school, and encourage them to improve their efforts to achieve the aims of the school.

*Mats Ekholm*

## References

ARVIDSSON, S. (1948) *Skolreformen. En sammanfattning av skolkommissionens betankande* Lund, Gleerups.

BAKER, K. (1980) 'Planning school policies for INSET: The SITE Project' in HOYLE, E. and MEGARRY, J. (Eds) *Professional Development of Teachers* London, Kogan Page.

EKHOLM, M. (1976) *Social Development in Schools. Summary and Excerpts* No. 48, Report from the Institute of Education, University of Goteborg, Goteborg.

EKHOLM, M. (1982) *The Development of Some Basic Attitudes of Democracy. Attitude Development During the School Years and a Ten Year Comparison* Linkoping, School Leader Education of Sweden.

EKHOLM, M. and SANDSTROM, B. (1983) *Studies of the Innovational Process in the Comprehensive School* Report from the Institute of Education, University of Linkoping, Linkoping.

GROSS, N., GIACQUINTA, J.B. and BERNSTEIN, M. (1971) *Implementing Organizational Innovation* New York, Harper and Row.

KEITH, P.M. and SMITH, L.M. (1971) *Anatomy of Educational Innovation.* New York, Wiley and Sons.

MILES, M.B. (1978) *Designing and Starting Innovative Schools: A Field Study of Social Architecture in Education. Executive Summary* New York, Center for Policy Research.

MURRAY, A.A. (1978) *Standard Provin Som Instrument Foer Jaenfoerelse AV Skolprestationes Pedagogiska Naemuden Redogoerelse Foer Verksamheton*, Stockholm, National Board of Education, p. 49–56.

PRATT, H., THURBER, J.C. and HALL, G.E. (1982) *Case Studies of School Improvement: A Concerns Based Approach.* Austin, Research and Development Center for Teacher Education.

SANDSTROM, B. (1983) *Lararnas syn pa skolan. Resultat av en intervjustudie.* Unpublished manuscript, Institute of Education, University of Linkoping, Linkoping.

SCHMUCK. R., MURRAY, D., SMITH, M., SCHWARTZ, M. and RUNKEL, M. (1975) *Consultation for Innovative Schools: OD for Multiunit Structures*, Eugene, Oregon, CEPM.

# Section Two:
# The Actors

*The four chapters in this section are critical to the underlying theme of the book because, ultimately, school improvement efforts are predicated on the behaviours of the actors involved in the situation. Each chapter in this section tackles an aspect of this theme.* **Jean Rudduck** *argues that school improvement cannot effectively occur without the involvement of students. Many innovations have failed because students have not internalized the meaning of a specific change, and it is important therefore to consider the students' perspective when initiating school improvement efforts.* **Lawrence Stenhouse** *takes the metaphor of the artist and applies it to teaching. This view implies that teachers need to develop a critical orientation towards their teaching, this being the way that the artist improves his/her practice.* **Bruce Joyce** *and* **Beverly Showers** *expand on this theme in their chapter on peer coaching. Drawing on the training research they argue that the most effective means of developing new teaching skills is through practice in the form of peer coaching. In other words teachers training each other, and assuming collective responsibility for professional development. Finally in this section* **Michael Fullan** *reviews the critical role of the principal as the gate keeper of educational change, and points to gaps in our knowledge of the principal's tasks. Taken as a whole the chapters in this section make a sustained argument for the consideration of roles played by pupils, teachers and principals in affecting school improvement.*

# Introducing Innovation to Pupils

Jean Rudduck
University of East Anglia

I have used the term 'innovation' in the title of this chapter but the task of defining innovation or classifying innovations is not easy. Let me begin by putting alongside the term "innovation', the terms 'development' and 'change'. In England, a colleague has coined the phrase 'innovation without change' to describe an experience of schools which have taken on the trappings of an innovation but not its spirit; they have subscribed to the rhetoric of innovation but not to the reality of change. This phrase suggests that innovation is the idea that lies outside the would-be innovators, and that change is the process they actually make towards the realization of that idea.

Schools and classrooms are of course likely to be in a constant state of development. Development may result from the diversity of unsung inputs from individual teachers and pupils. Development rests on small change events, none of which is threatening in itself to the whole structure; on the contrary, each event, though it acts as a minute impulse for change, confirms the known past. Innovation is different: it is conscious, planned, and involves some fundamental breaks with the known past (Hull and Rudduck, 1980). In referring to 'innovation' in this chapter, I have in mind something that if realized, would require among those involved a substantial shift from the pattern of their present practices.

In the last ten years we have made rapid progress in constructing a map that records our understanding of the process of change in schools. This book demonstrates how studies conducted relatively independently in Canada, in Australia, in the USA, in Europe and in Britain are confirming the main features of the landscape of innovation. But there is one area of this map that has not been explored at all systematically. The area I am talking about is the area of pupils and innovation: including the power of pupils in relation to the progress of an innovation in schools and classrooms; and the problems that pupils face as conscripts in the innovative campaigns launched by teachers and schools.

Why is it that we have given so little attention to these issues in our attempts to study and understand the process of change in schools? I shall start by recording some of the insights offered in a SITE lecture which underline the strangeness of this neglect. Bruce Joyce talked about the problems of incorporation that innovations present to teachers. In particular he emphasized the difficulty of integrating new skills or new perspectives into a pattern of behaviour that is already well established and complex in its interrelationships. He then reviewed the difficulties teachers have in operating new skills or new perspectives in situations that have become associated with the old skills and the old perspectives: habits are easy, comfortable and anxiety free. Bruce Joyce also mentioned the need for 'deprogramming' a teacher, and he mentioned the dislocation of the teacher's routines. He went on to talk about the need for the community to recognize that an innovation that requires substantial change of habit among teachers is likely to impose on teachers the burden of incompetence while they experiment with and learn to feel comfortable with the new skills. The community, he argues, needs to see the necessity of this period of experimentation, and to be prepared to legitimize tentativeness, uncertainty, and temporary incompetence. In this way, innovating teachers may sense a context of support, and they may have the nerve to see the innovation through. As Bruce Joyce memorably put it: the community must be understanding of, and tolerant of, the 'socially deviant behaviour' which teachers are likely to exhibit in the early stages of any fairly substantial innovation.

Bruce Joyce is here confirming, in vivid fashion, our own experience in England of the problems of innovation, but I want to ask: should we not be extending these observations about teachers to pupils? Does not the innovation dislocate the routines of pupils as well as teachers? And is not the dislocation of routine as uneasy an experience for pupils as it is for teachers? Does not innovation disorient and deskill pupils as well as teachers? And if we need to legitimize teachers' tentativeness and insecurity as new ways of working are introduced in the classroom, should we not also think how to help pupils see that uncertainty and tentativeness may be legitimate – whether it is their own or the teacher's – and that insecurity may be natural to the situation at that point in time?

At this stage I would like to offer an illustration of the problems of disorientation and dislocation that an innovation may pose for pupils. The comments were made by fourteen year old pupils in classes where the teachers were trying to develop discussion as a way of learning, and were trying to move away from the role of instructor and authority which the pupils and they were familiar with. One pupil said this:

> All our life, we have been in schools. We've been taught that what the teacher says is right. But when we're in this room doing discussion, it's hard for us to disagree with him after all these years. We sort of come to conform with them.

Another pupil said this: 'Discussion's not work.' Another pupil said that she thought the teacher, who was trying to act as a chairperson, must have lost her voice or be feeling ill because she wasn't talking all the time as she usually did! Another pupil said he wouldn't talk unless the teacher, who had starting sitting among the pupils in a circle of chairs, got back behind the bars of his desk!

The thesis that I want to explore in this chapter is this: that where innovations fail to take root in schools and classrooms, it may be because pupils are guardians of the existing culture, and as such represent a powerful conservative force in the classroom; and that unless we give attention to the problems that pupils face, we may be overlooking a significant feature of the innovation process.

Bruce Joyce talked about the community exerting a homeostatic influence on the culture of the school – and he defined the community in terms of parents and administrators. I want to argue that it is the community in the classroom – the pupils – that may be exerting the strongest influence towards stability, and not surprisingly so, if we fail, as we often have done in the past, to involve pupils in understanding the purpose and the process of the change that the teacher or the school is intent on bringing about.

I am at the moment involved in a research project that started from these premises [Social Science Research Council Project: 'The effects of systematic induction conferences for pupils on pupils' perceptions of an innovation. (Grant no. 6841/1)] and which asked the question: if we think it is important to run inservice training courses for teachers, to help them understand and implement an innovation, should we also arrange such opportunities for pupils? After all, pupils are partners in the educational transactions of the school and the classroom, and they are just as much subject to the pressures of routine and convention as are their teachers.

In this section of the chapter, I have outlined the theme and tried to justify it. Before developing the theme I would like to describe how I became increasingly aware of its potential importance.

## Illustration

There are three events that marked the stages of my interest and awareness. The first occurred when I visited an open plan primary school in England a few months after it had opened. The pupils had been transferred, with their teachers, from an old Victorian school with dark classrooms and heavy desks and with an atmosphere quite different from the atmosphere of the new school. I talked to the school principal who said that the teachers had adjusted well to the new situation – they had had considerable support in terms of discussions and opportunities to attend courses to prepare them for the transition – but that the pupils had had some difficulty. Pupils had started to steal pencils and to hide them away in little personal caches. The school staff became concerned about this phenomenon and met to try to interpret it and plan what to do. Their interpretation was that pupils were missing the sense of possession over space that they had in their old school where they worked in their own classrooms and could put their belongings in their own desks. The staff thought that by hiding pencils away in secret places, the pupils, who were five or six years old, would feel that they had a private space in the school which they could think of as their own. The school principal and her staff decided to flood the school with pencils until children felt less under threat by the openness of their environment. I was struck, in this event, by the way in which the problems that the teachers might encounter in this transition had been anticipated whereas the problems that the pupils might encounter had not.

The next event was a story told me by a student teacher; it related to her first teaching practice. She was working with a class of five year old pupils in a school which had decided, for the first time, to celebrate the coming of the autumn by holding a harvest festival. The pupils became increasingly excited as they brought in fruit, vegetables, bread and flowers and arranged them in the main hall of the school. Every morning they would ask: 'When will it be harvest festival?' One afternoon the pupils were taken into the hall where they sat on the floor in rows and listened to the minister who talked to them for about half an hour. The next morning the children continued to ask: 'When will it be harvest festival?' But harvest festival, as the teachers knew, was the occasion of the talk, in the hall, by the minister. The idea in the minds of the teachers, which they had taken for granted, had not been explained to the pupils.

The third story, which I want to tell in some detail, relates to a curriculum development project on which I worked as a member of the project's central team. The project was called 'The Humanities Curriculum Project' (HCP) and was directed by Lawrence Stenhouse. About four years after the project was officially 'over' – that is, its period of financial support had ceased and the project was well into its phase of dissemination – Lawrence Stenhouse and I decided that we would like to take a fresh look at the project and we asked the principal of a comprehensive secondary school near the university where we worked whether we could have a group of fourteen or fifteen year old pupils for two periods a week for at least two terms. Now, to make sense of this story, I have to say something about this project as 'an innovation'. The project's evaluator, Barry MacDonald, observed at the start of the project's dissemination that HCP exhibited all the characteristics of a case study in the pathology of innovation: it was difficult to understand; it was costly in terms of school resources; it conflicted with the established values of most classrooms. In this project, discussion was the main mode of inquiry and the teacher acted as a neutral chairperson. Discussion was informed and disciplined by evidence: that is, items of material from history, journalism, literature, philosophy, art, photography, statistics might be introduced if they were relevant in order to help the pupils extend the range of their considerations and to deepen their understanding of the issue under discussion. Here are summarized the kinds of demand which this curriculum project made on teachers, pupils and schools:

*New skills for most teachers*
1   Discussion rather than instruction.
2   Teacher as neutral chairperson – that is, not communicating his or her point of view.
3   Teacher talk reduced to about 15%.
4   Teacher handling material from different disciplines.
5   New modes of assessment.

*New skills for most pupils*
1   Discussion, not argument or debate.
2   Listening to, and talking to, each other, not just to the teacher.
3   Taking initiatives in contributing – not being cued in by teacher.

### New content for many classrooms

1  Explorations of controversial social issues, often in the sensitive areas (e.g. race relations, poverty, family, relations between the sexes).
2  Evidence reproduced in an original form – no simplifications of language.

### Organizational demands on schools

1  Small discussion groups, each with teacher chairperson.
2  Mixed ability groups found by many schools to be desirable.
3  Non-row formation of chairs – circle or rectangle appearing to be desirable.

The project team put much effort into helping teachers understand the principles of the project through attendance at rigorously planned and intensive residential training courses. Although we were aware that pupils had difficulty in making adjustments to this way of learning, we gave remarkably little attention to the task of helping teachers introduce the innovation to pupils. Our evaluation officer was aware of the problem, however: he said (MacDonald, 1973:24):

> Teachers do not anticipate the extent to which pupils have developed, in their previous schooling, a trained incapacity for this work, nor the degree to which the pupils have been successfully socialized into a tradition of teacher dominance and custodial attitudes.

It was not until I experienced directly, as a teacher in the classroom might experience it, the problem of introducing this innovation to pupils that I began to appreciate the practical and theoretical implications.

Back to my third story. Lawrence Stenhouse and I were given a group of twenty, fourteen year old pupils for a double period a week – about seventy minutes. The sessions were scheduled on Monday morning immediately before the lunch break. The pupils would normally have been doing English literature. In the school the pupils were streamed for some subjects and in the fourth year there were ten streams. We were given the ninth stream – a mixture of pupils who knew that they were almost bottom but who had not quite given up hope, and pupils who were able but who had in spirit given up school. The teacher who normally taught them was having severe discipline problems with the group and gladly surrendered them to us and to the Humanities Curriculum Project. Incidentally, the school had tried the project six years ago but had abandoned it because the teachers found it too difficult. Project materials were lying in cupboards, laced with cobwebs.

Lawrence and I arrived one Monday morning. A teacher explained to the whole group of pupils that they were to work in smaller groups, one with Mr. Stenhouse and one with Miss Rudduck 'from the university'. The group lists were read out. The principle of allocation was not made clear although we were told later, and the pupils must have known, that all the really tough and unruly pupils were put in Lawrence's group – I had the rest. Our meetings were to be held in the block reserved exclusively for the use of the senior pupils in the school – the seventeen and eighteen year olds. Unlike the ordinary classrooms, which had rows of desks, the rooms we were to use were fairly small and had chairs around in a central block of tables; the only familiar feature of the new classroom was the blackboard. The pupils we were to work with had so far no experience in school of working through discussion.

So began our attempt at innovation – under not very auspicious circumstances, but circumstances that many other teachers attempting the innovation would have found themselves facing. We started. Each week I began the session by explaining that I was acting as a chairperson, not a teacher; the discussion was an opportunity to learn from each other and not from me; that there was evidence which we could use to help that discussion along and give it depth. The group listened, apparently attentively, for this bit was familiar: it was teacher talk. But they didn't ask questions about what I meant nor seemed to relate what I had said to what followed. After a few weeks they had learned to write the title, Humanities Curriculum Project, on their folders, and spell it correctly. This again was a familiar achievement.

My acting as a chairperson and sitting at the table alongside the pupils marked a change from the conventional authority-based relationship of teacher and taught. But the pupils had no conception of any alternative convention for they could not realize the form of discussion for a long enough period of time to perceive what the structure of the alternative convention might be. In this limbo world, behaviours that would normally be suppressed, or if expressed would constitute a direct challenge to the authority of the teacher, were given free range. In adopting the role of the chairperson I had cut myself off from the usual means of control that the behaviour of the group would certainly have elicited in a normal teaching situation. There was an impulse towards small talk and against this backdrop of perpetual and seemingly mindless motion there stood out a number of attention-seeking incidents which custom never seemed to stale. We seemed to have arrived at an impasse in terms of progress with discussion. Maintaining my role was a severe strain. I could understand why teachers might give up. We recorded each discussion on audio-tape and the group was interested in playing back the tape – but only to hear the sound of their own voices or to have a go at being in charge of the technology. There were some achievements in the handling of discussion, but they were not cumulative, and I couldn't see how to advance the learning in any systematic way. And then came the big breakthrough.

One week we invited both our groups down to the university to watch video-tapes of pupils in other schools attempting the same style of work. To be honest, I think at the time we had conceived this as an outing rather than as an opportunity to test an educational hypothesis. It was a relief from the strain of trying to sustain the innovation. The pupils assembled; we gave them coffee and biscuits. The chauvinist impulses that had made it difficult for girls to contribute at all to the discussion without ridicule were now apparent in the social organization of the group. Girls sat at the back, boys sat near the TV screen and ate the biscuits. The first video-tape we put on was a disaster in that it unwittingly played to these chauvinist tendencies. It was made in an all girls school. Now, in an all girls school there is no incentive for girls to display to boys. There they sat on the screen, hair in untidy bunches, glasses on the ends of their noses, wearing lumpish pullovers. Our boys had never known a situation in class in which there was not an element of sexual awareness: our girls wore black bras under white blouses; their make-up was subtle. The tape represented an unfamiliar and absurd world. The group was hysterical. We had to take off the tape.

The second video-tape was more productive. Our pupils started to respond, making comments on the size of the group, the seating arrangements – in both cases similar to the ones we had adopted. They also noted the teacher's generally short and quiet contributions.

Next week, in my group, the climate had changed. Jim was speaking for the group – and Jim was also the group leader. He was the guardian of the old regime. What I would like to quote now is a memorable passage from that next session. We were discussing an issue within the theme, relations between the sexes, and considering the circumstance of early marriages and arranged marriages:

*Jim*   Miss is talking too much and getting interested in the
        group. As chairman she shouldn't talk, you know, as much,

leaving it to the group to argue between themselves. Well, not sort of argue – to talk between themselves and have more discussion between themselves than with the teacher. Because you are, you know, sort of being the chairman and not the teacher.

*Ellen*   Miss, this Indian's mother went back to India and brought back a husband while her daughter was still in the sixth form.

*Me*   (An interested response) Really?

*Jim*   There you go again Miss.

*Me*   (Slightly apologetically and rather illogically) I'm trying to ask a question.

*Jim*   Oi, you lot! Instead of talking to Miss, talk between us lot. Everything you say, you say to Miss. Why don't you talk between us lot?

The opinion leader in the group had become the interpreter of the innovation, not the saboteur of the innovation.

This experience has been recounted in such detail for two reasons. First, to suggest the complexity – the tight weave – of settings which an innovation tries to enter and where it tries to take hold. Second, to expose four hypotheses which I now think are worth exploring with teachers in other schools where fundamental changes to classroom pedagogy or to the organization of school life and learning are being attempted.

1   Pupils' understanding of the form of the innovation will be increased if they have access to concrete representations of the form in addition to oral explanation.

2   If an innovation requires a substantial shift in classroom roles and relationships, teacher and pupils will have to develop a mutual commitment to the work which will counter the pull of existing conventions.

3   The development of a mutual commitment by teacher and pupils requires understanding of the nature of the innovation and negotation about the management of classroom control (negotiation may be implicit rather than explicit).

4   Alertness on the part of the teacher to aspects of the task of communicating the nature of the innovation to pupils will

increase the likelihood of the innovation taking root in the classroom.

## Reflection

At this point I should like to review and elaborate on the issues that give meaning to the story I have just told. First, there is the acknowledgement that pupils' definitions of school and classroom behaviour can be powerful conservative forces in educational practice. If the norms of classroom behaviour are suddenly changed and a new mode of learning introduced – with the Humanities Project it was the inquiry mode, with discussion as the main vehicle for learning, with the teacher acting as a neutral chairperson, and with unconventional seating patterns – then it is not surprising that the pupils might seek to reinstate the familiar, the comfortably predictable, and through the power of group pressure lure the teacher back into recognizable routines.

Second, we need to think therefore on what basis innovations are introduced to pupils. In Ted Aoki's words, within the instrumental model of implementation, an innovation is likely to be perceived by teacher and pupil as a new commodity to be dispensed by teachers and consumed by pupils. In such a framework, teachers are likely to construe the introduction of an innovation as the implementation of a set of practices which their authority, or the authority of the school, is sufficient to enforce. Pupils are unlikely to be helped to understand the meaning of the innovation: that is, what the innovation implies for teacher-pupil and pupil-pupil relationships in the classroom; what different behaviours or kinds of achievement will be valued; the view of knowledge that the innovation endorses. Instead pupils may have to build up the jigsaw of meaning from the pieces of information which their observation of the teacher's behaviour, over time, will yield – and if pupils do not have the curiosity or patience to puzzle things out, then they may choose instead to resist the innovation and escape from uncertainty by moving back onto the familiar territory of established norms. An alternative to the imposition of an innovation through the authority of the teacher is to negotiate the meaning of the innovation with pupils. What Ted Aoki said fits well: in his practical action model of implementation he talked about a 'communal venturing forth' together to understand the meaning of the new structure in which both teacher and pupils are to work; indeed, the critical exploration of that meaning is, he said, a precondition of effective acting together.

Third, we have to find a way in which to set up and conduct this critical dialogue. Originally, we (Hull and Rudduck, 1980) had conceptualized the task in this way:

> For planned innovation to be successful, the pedagogical model in the minds of the designers of the innovation must become transparently real to the members of the target culture. This is often a staged process. Once the teacher has interpreted the pedagogical model in the minds of the designers of the innovation, the model in the mind of the teacher must become transparently real to the pupils.

Aoki put it differently: the teacher may invite her pupils to enter her interpretative framework and to sort out the meaning of the innovation in dialogue.

But this is easier said than done. How is this to be achieved? Our experience suggests that explanations of principle are inadequate to convey the meaning of an innovation to pupils if the pupils have no reference points in their past experience which will allow them to translate those principles into dynamic behaviours. In the long anecdote which I offered earlier, pupils had no shared referent for such abstract terms as 'neutral chairperson; 'discussion', 'pupil initiative', 'reflective inquiry'. They realized these concepts in action almost accidentally, it seemed, from time to time, but they could not sustain the form of learning long enough to analyze it and explore its meaning collaboratively. If an explanation of principles is inadequate, pupils need an illustration of the principles in practice. Hence our shift towards video-tapes of other groups of pupils engaged in work which embodies those principles. Video-tape, we think, may have two strengths. First, it legitimizes the involvement of pupils and teachers in the innovation. They see other groups, in recognizable school situations, behaving in the 'abnormal' way of the innovation. In the often conventional climates of schools this can be helpful. It is a way of legitimizing what Bruce Joyce called the 'socially deviant behaviour' of an innovation. Second, video-tape provides a shared image of the 'abnormal' behaviour of the innovation which can be analyzed by the group, and out of this analysis the group may come to build their own sense of form. What I am trying to say here is that the principles of an innovation are best communicated through a shared experience of the principles in action, and if this cannot be achieved within the group itself, then it may be attempted through a surrogate experience of the principles in action which video-tape can supply.

*Jean Rudduck*

## A Broader Framework

At this point I would like to move out from this close-up concern with one small but potentially significant aspect of change in schools and try to fit what I have been talking about into a broader framework.

In this framework the key concept is culture. Hagerstrand, from Sweden, who has written about the spatial diffusion of innovations from the standpoint of a geographer, defined an innovation as a 'cultural novelty'. This for me was a beguiling definition – but what do we mean by 'culture'? Culture is a social accomplishment; it is learned and shared. Culture is about the capability of the members of a group to act on the basis of a consensus of meanings manifested in linguistic usage and dependent on a deeper consensus of values and understandings (Stenhouse, 1963, p. 122). The power of culture is that it can sustain a complex pattern of norms. We can see that this is so at the level of the classroom in the anecdote that I told earlier. Michael Olmsted confirms this in his book, *The Small Group* (1959:84):

> Each group (that is, a class in school) has a subculture of its own, a selected and modified version of some thoughts of the larger culture (that is, the school) . . . without its own culture no group would be more than a plurality, a congeries of individuals. The common meanings, the definitions of the situation, the norms of belief and behaviour – all these go to make up the culture of the group.
>
> (my parentheses)

This would be true for any other working group.

It seems helpful, therefore, to analyze the problems of innovation in terms of cultural change (see Rudduck, 1976, 1977). The task in innovation is to penetrate the existing culture of the group and to create a new culture from within. The main difficulty, as we have seen, is that one cannot establish a temporary cultural vacuum in order to make space for what is new. Nor, indeed, if one could eliminate the existing culture, would there be a basis for exploring, collaboratively, the meaning of innovation.

In the era of curriculum development, which was characterized by the setting-up of large-scale curriculum projects, there was little recognition, nor perhaps could there be, of the significance of this aspect of the process of innovation. The concern to grapple with the meaning of an innovation with a working group – whether the staff of the school, a team of teachers, or a teacher and a class of pupils – may have been baulked by the conditions which the centralized structure for planned change imposed. First, as Sarason (1971) points out in *The Culture of the School and The Problem of Change* the designers of the innovation or the agents of the designer – the disseminators whose task it is to make contact with the teachers – often have little knowledge or understanding of the school situation. Sarason (1971: 7–8) comments:

> Many people having a role in, or concern for, educational planning and change possess no intimate knowledge of the culture of the setting they wish to influence or change ... many of the people involved have little or no basis, either in theory, or in experience, for understanding the structure of the school, its traditions and its usual ways of accommodating to change.

There was, therefore, little basis in the encounters between disseminators and schools for developing a language in which the meaning of an innovation could be explored. Instead, disseminators seem to have become increasingly preoccupied with the management of innovation and with measuring the impact of an innovation or the level of use of an innovation (Rudduck, 1980).

Sarason also comments on the convention of the large-scale curriculum development projects of the 1960s and 1970s where the disseminators of an innovation were often content, at regional in-service courses for example, to deal with individual representatives of the innovating institution rather than with a working group – thereby demonstrating, in my view, an insensitivity to the cultural implications of change and to the power of the group as the guardian of existing cultural patterns. At least, I think this is what Sarason (1971:59) is getting at when he writes:

> In practice, most explicit and implicit perceptions of change derive from the language and vocabulary of an individual psychology that is in no way adequate to changing social settings.

What I am trying to say here is that the negotiation of new meanings, or shared meanings, is at the heart of the process of innovation and that the models of diffusion that we use must be appropriate both to the conditions of schools and to the cultural import of innovations.

*Jean Rudduck*

## Summary

Culture is the medium which allows members of the group to communicate within a consensus of meaning. In the interactions of the school or classroom it is difficult to introduce a complex innovation, which requires substantial shifts of habit and perspective, without taking into account the power of the existing culture and without giving attention to the task of negotiating a new set of shared understandings as a condition of collaborative action within the working group. Pupils are in partnership with teachers in the everyday educational transactions of the school and classroom, and attempts at planned innovation must aim therefore to help both teachers and pupils move out of the comfortable cradle of convention and accept a period of exploration and negotiation in order to interpret the meaning of the innovative possibility which lies before them and to realize that meaning in action.

## References

HULL, C. and RUDDUCK, J. (1980) *Introducing Innovation to Pupils* A paper given at the AERA Annual Meeting, Boston, April.

MacDONALD, B. (1973) 'Briefing decision makers' in HAMINGSON, D. (Ed) *Towards Judgement*, CARE Occasional Publications No.1, University of East Anglia, pp. 12–36.

OLMSTED, M.S. (1959) *The Small Group*, New York, Random House.

RUDDUCK, J. (1976) 'Dissemination as acculturation research', *Social Science Research Council Newsletter* 32 October, pp. 7–10.

RUDDUCK, J. (1977) 'Dissemination as the encounter of cultures', *Research Intelligence* 3 (1) pp. 3–5.

RUDDUCK, J. (1980) *Curriculum Dissemination as Planned Cultural Diffusion* A paper given at the AERA Annual Meeting, Boston, April.

SARASON, S.B. (1971) *The Culture of the School and the Problem of Change* Boston, Allyn and Bacon.

STENHOUSE, L. (1963) 'A cultural approach to the sociology of the curriculum', *Pedagogisk Forskning* Nordisk Tidsskrift for Pedagogik, pp. 120–134.

# Artistry and Teaching: The Teacher as Focus of Research and Development

Lawrence Stenhouse
University of East Anglia

Experience tells me that if I am not to be misunderstood I must begin this chapter by offering you a brief sketch of my views on the relation of research to educational action. These views are set out at a greater length in other works (Stenhouse 1979, 1980, 1983).

There is in England a strong doctrine that the study of education is fed by the contributory disciplines of history, philosophy, and sociology. I agree that these disciplines do contribute to our understanding of education. In my own personal experience I can say that in the curriculum project with which I am most closely associated, the Humanities Curriculum Project, my own contribution was substantially influenced by my knowledge of the history of elementary school readers (that is, text books), of the philosophical work of R S Peters, of the social psychology of groups, and of the sociology of knowledge. These disciplines, while they serve to stimulate educational imagination and to define the conditions of educational action, do not serve to guide such action. They provide for education – as rules of the game and traditions of play do for a sport – a context in which to plan intelligent action. But they do not tell us how to act.

The yearning towards a form of research which might guide educational action led educational researchers to look enviously at agricultural research. Here, in a tradition associated with Ronald Fisher, researchers had conducted field trials which utilized random sampling in block and plot designs in order to recommend to farmers those strains of seed and crop treatments which would maximize yield. Both random sampling – which legitimized the deployment of the statistics of probability to estimate error and significance – and the measure of yield present problems in educational research. A number of classic papers, among which Campbell and Stanley's 'Experimental and Quasi-Experimental Designs for Research in Teaching' (1963) is prominent, have considered the robustness of various experimental designs and statistical procedures in terms of reliability and validity as sampling falls away from the desideratum of randomness. The doctrine of behavioural objectives allied to the development of criterion-referenced testing was developed to give measure of educational yield.

Personally, I am satisfied that the application of this so-called 'psycho-statistical paradigm' (Fienberg 1977) in educational research provides no reliable guide to action (though it may contribute a little to theory). It has to assume, as agriculturalists assume in treating a crop in a field, consistency of treatment throughout the treatment group; but it is the teacher's job to work like a gardener rather than a farmer, differentiating the treatment of each subject and each learner as the gardener does each flower bed and each plant. The variability of educational situations is grossly underestimated: sampling procedures cannot be related to educational action except on a survey basis rather than an experimental basis. Further, behavioural objectives are quite inappropriate to education except in the case of skill learning. They are a monument to the philosophical naivete of a psychological tradition which simplifies intentionality and purpose to 'having a goal'. Purpose in education is about having an agenda.

Now, if I am right about this – and you will not readily persuade me that I am not – then the question arises: if experimental research based on sampling cannot tell us how to act in education, how are we as teachers to know what to do?

One answer to this question is that instructions shall be laid down for us in the form of curricula and specifications of teaching methods. I reject this. Education is learning in the context of a search for truth. Truth cannot be defined by the state even through democratic processes: close control of curricula and teaching methods in schools is to be likened to the totalitarian control of art. Reaching towards the truth through education is a matter of situational professional judgement; and professors of education or administrators cannot tell us what we should be doing. Prescriptions will vary according to cases. We do not need doctors if all they are going to give us is a treatment laid down by the state or suggested by their professor without bothering to examine us and make a diagnosis.

Educational action is concerned with varying according to case and to context the pursuit of truth through learning. In this subtle and complicated process, how is the teacher to conceive the problem: what shall I do? This riddle provides the context and occasion of my chapter.

The student who, during the course of ten years in school, meets two or three outstanding and congenial teachers has had a fortunate educational experience. Many are not so lucky.

The improvement of schooling hinges on increasing the numbers of outstanding teachers, on serving their needs, and on trying to ensure that their virtues are not frustrated by the system. The basic institutional frameworks of the educational enterprise – the neighbourhood elementary school and the comprehensive high school – are for the moment stably established or well on the way. Within these frameworks it is the outstanding teachers who transmute the process of instruction into the adventure of education. Others, it is true, may teach us; but it is *they* who teach us to delight in learning and to exult in the extension of powers that learning gives.

As part of a National Science Foundation Study of the status of science education in United States schools, Bob Stake and Jack Easley of the University of Illinois directed a collection of 'Case Studies in Science Education' (1978). Eleven close case studies of high schools and their feeder elementaries in different states were followed up by a national survey. One of their major conclusions confirmed the stance I have just taken. The science teaching that students received was good to the extent that they met good science teachers: teachers who, being interested in science, were absorbed by and skilful in teaching it.

That good teaching is created by good teachers may to some of you seem self-evident to the point of absurdity. You don't need eleven case studies across the American nation – or me to fly to Vancouver from Norwich – to tell you that. But the implications of this self-evident proposition do not seem to be widely grasped.

Good teachers are necessarily autonomous in professional judgement. They do not need to be told what to do. They are not professionally the dependents of researchers or superintendents, of innovators or supervisors. This does not mean that they do not welcome access to ideas created by other people at other places or in other times. Nor do they reject advice, consultancy or support. But they do know that ideas and people are not of much real use until they are digested to the point where they are subject to the teacher's own judgement. In short, it is the task of all educationalists outside the classroom to serve the teachers; for only teachers are in the position to create good teaching.

Let me restate my case by saying that I am declaring teaching an art; and then elaborate on that. By an art I mean an exercise of skill expressive of meaning. The painter, the poet, the musician, the actor and the dancer all express meaning through skill. Some artists fly so high that we designate them geniuses, and that may be true of some teachers. But a claim as ambitious as that does not need to be made on behalf of the excellent teachers I have spoken of. It is enough that they have assiduously cultivated modest but worthwhile talents like those of the innumerable stonemasons who adorned the English parish churches or those sound repertory actors who exceed in number the jobs the theatre has to offer. In short I am not elevating teachers inordinately. Rather I am diagnosing the nature of their job in order to discern how performances may be improved. I am suggesting that just as dramatists, theatre school staff, producers, stage managers, front of house managers and even booking agencies need to understand to some degree the players' art, so curriculum developers, educational researchers, teacher educators, supervisors and administrators need to understand the art of the teacher.

Teaching is the art which expresses in a form accessible to learners an understanding of the nature of that which is to be learned. Thus, teaching music is about understanding the nature of music and having the skill to teach it true to one's understanding. Teaching tennis is about understanding the logic and psychology and techniques of the game and about expressing that understanding through skill in teaching. Similarly, the teaching of French expresses an understanding of the nature of language and culture and of that particular language and culture; the teaching of wrought ironwork as a craft expresses the relationship of material to fitness for use and to concepts of beauty; and so forth. And one mainstream tradition of teaching is an expression of knowledge of a discipline or field of knowledge; it is always to 'teach' the epistemology of that discipline, the nature of its tenure on knowledge.

My own belief, as I have said, is that whether teaching is concerned with that knowledge we associate with the disciplines or with the arts or with practical skills, it should aspire to express a view of knowledge or of a field of activity. This epistemological desideratum might be expressed by saying that the teacher should aspire to give learners access to insight into the status of what they learn. The way towards this is that a view of knowledge comes to infuse the teacher's perception of subject matter and judgement of the performance of students, and that this view and its status becomes revealed, by teaching, to the student. Such a perception of knowledge develops and deepens throughout the career of a good teacher and it is the product of the teacher's personal construction or reconstruction of knowledge. It can be assisted by reading and instruction, but it is essentially a personal construction created from socially available resources and it cannot be imparted by others or to others in a straightforward manner.

Now, the construction of a personal perception of our world from the knowledge and traditions that our culture makes available to us is a task that faces not only the teacher, but also the student; and teaching rests on both partners in the process being at different stages of the same enterprise. This is clear to us when we watch a great musician teaching a master class, but it tends to be obscured in schools in the ordinary classroom. The technical claptrap of learning systems and behavioural objectives is much to blame for this. Good learning is about making, not mere doing. It is about constructing a view of the world. It is not about showing that, although you have failed in that construction, you are capable of all the performances that would appear to make the construction possible. Education is for real: it is not (to borrow an image from Bruce Joyce) about practice shots.

Let me sum up so far by an analogy (which is not be pursued too far). The art of social comedy expresses a view of manners and morals as people live them: the art of education expresses a view of knowledge as people live it. The medium of one is theatrical entertainment; of the other, schooling. Both are at their highest when the audience or learner is brought to reflect consciously on the message he or she receives. This fulfilment depends not only upon the quality of the play or the curriculum, but also upon the art of the actor or teacher.

And now let me take a second step. All good art is an inquiry and an experiment. It is by virtue of being an artist that the teacher is a researcher. The point appears to be difficult to grasp because education faculties have been invaded by the idea that research is scientific and concerned with general laws. This notion persists even though our universities teach music and literature and history and art and lay an obligation on their staff in these fields to conduct research. Why then should research in education look only to science?

The artist is the researcher *par excellence*. So much so that prominent scientists are now arguing that, while routine consolidation in science can be achieved by following conventional scientific method, the big breakthroughs really show that science is an art. I am sceptical of that, but I am clear that all art rests upon research and the purpose of the artist's research is to improve the truth of his performance. Leonardo's sketchbooks, George Stubbs dissecting a horse in his studio, Nureyev working with a partner in a new ballet, Solti and the Chicago Symphony Orchestra tackling Beethoven, Derek Jacobi evolving his Hamlet, all are engaged in inquiry, in research and development of their own work. And this development, though it involves improvement of technique, is not for the sake of technique: it is for the sake of the expression of a truth in a performance which challenges criticism in those terms.

Thus, an elementary school teacher who wishes to improve his or her teaching of science will record teaching or invite a colleague in as an observer, and will, if possible, bring in an outsider to monitor the children's perceptions as a basis for 'triangulation'. From this the next aspiration is to drop the outsider and move towards open discourse between teacher and children about the teaching/learning process in the classroom and its 'meaning'. A crucial aspect of this meaning is the impression of science – always expressed in specific instances or episodes – that the children are acquiring. And this the teacher needs to criticize in the light of the philosophy of science. All teaching falsifies its subject as it shapes it into the form of teaching and learning: the art of pedagogy is to minimize the falsification of knowledge. It is the aspiration to do this, to shape understanding without distortion into pedagogic forms that is the challenge to develop one's art.

Now, if you say that most teachers are not like this, I shall reply that some are, and that it is the model of teaching that those teachers display to us that we need to disseminate. Allow me here to be a little of the wild-eyed maniac whose intervention Bruce Joyce sanctioned in his SITE lecture. The way ahead is to disseminate the idea of teacher as artist with the implication that artists exercise autonomy of judgement founded upon research directed towards improvement in their art. The changes in school administration or curriculum or teaching arrangements which will be required are those which make it possible to implement that vision.

If I, as a teacher, absorb and accept the case I have just been putting, then it is clear to me that I am the focus of research and development. Who else could be? My problem then is how to get others to recognise it. That is not going to be easy. If teachers are at the bottom of the pile, there are bound to be lots of people who like it that way. So, though I can exercise my art in secret, or even in a small group of consenting adults, if I want the support of a movement, I need to make alliances and develop some political power.

Let me give you a short account of the kinds of support that have been developed round the teacher-as-researcher movement in Britain. There is an alliance between some universities or colleges of education and some teacher groups. What is required of the universities is that they break the stranglehold of the 'psycho-statistical and nomothetic paradigm' on educational research. The universities which have done this recognize forms of research alternative to the still dominant tradition of scientific positivism with its emphasis on experimental and survey procedures conducted on samples in field settings and giving rise to 'results'. Among these alternative forms are experimental or descriptive case studies which may be based upon the teacher's access either to the classroom as a laboratory or to the school or classroom as a setting for participant observation. In Britain standards for these research paradigms are now in process of being worked out at master's and doctoral levels, both through discussion at conferences and in the consultations between internal and external examiners.

This alliance with universities is important for the teachers because it gives access to a pattern of part-time study right up to the level of the doctorate which turns one towards one's professional work rather than away from it and offers a systematic training in the appropriate research skills as well as a grasp of the theoretical issues applicable to close-in, practitioner research. This tradition, once established at advanced levels, begins to influence patterns of in-service work.

Academic validation has drawn on alternative traditions which include the hermeneutic tradition and the neo-Marxist tradition from Germany, phenomenology and ethnomethodology. These theoretical currents are in harmony with reappraisals at present being conducted in the social science community whose interests lie outside education. This link is a source of validation and alliance. It turns the education faculty towards sociologists, anthropologists and historians as alternative allies to psychologists and philosophers. This shift of alliance has, of course, profound power implications in the academic community.

The academic endorsement of styles of research into schooling which are as accessible to practising school teachers as to university teachers and professional researchers can also, of course, create considerable hostility and fear among university faculty. In my view, this is misplaced. The universities can only thrive the more as a result of an extension of the boundaries of the research community. The shift is from lecturing on research results towards training researchers. There is room for both, of course, but the balance becomes different. The message is that the 'role' of universities is bound to be central in the development of a tradition that puts research at its heart.

Of course, teacher power expresses itself in unfamiliar ways within this tradition. The Schools Council for Curriculum and Examinations, the main funding agency for curriculum in Britain recently funded a conference of teachers on 'The Teacher as Researcher' (Nixon, 1981). The teachers who organized it did not invite anyone from a university. I guess we talk too much, and they wanted time to think over the issues in their own way. But they will need us; and we need them. In an age of accountability, educational research will be held accountable for its relevance to practice, and that relevance can only be validated by practitioners.

Enlightened administrators look benevolently on the teacher-researcher model of staff development, and one can gather support there. The idea has potential appeal for teacher unions, though that hasn't really been pressed home in Britain. One way or another there are the makings of a movement.

But what are the consequences to be expected of such a movement if it gathers momentum and power? May we expect teachers to demand schools fit for educational artist-researchers to live in? And what would those look like?

We can only guess. But I am suggesting that forms of schooling can best be seen as obsolescent when they constrict developments in teaching. I believe that the development of the teacher as artist means that some time in the future we are going to have to get rid of school principals. My own guess is that we shall need delegatory rather than legislative democracy. Committees will not decide what to do: artists grudge that use of time. They will delegate the power to decide to individuals for fixed periods and will hold them accountable. In the University in which I work professors who run departments or faculties are no different from those who teach or do research: their leadership role is more an award than an appointment. A capacity for intellectual leadership is appropriate, but the leadership role is not structured on the job. Perhaps we need such a concept in schools: persons appointed by their colleagues to a status which recognizes their distinctive capacity to contribute to the community of teachers.

A community of teachers whose attention is primarily focused on the art of teaching will require – as a company of actors does or as a university faculty does – an administrative support structure. It is important that the teacher who acts as president of the school faculty commands the highest salary in the institution, and below that the head of the administration has parity with the highest grade of teacher. It is vital that administrators service teaching, not lead it.

However, we shall not change teaching by creating a school organized on that model. The reform of school organization needs to be an adjustment to the development of teaching. It is the teacher who is the focus of research and development: only the teacher can change the teacher. You can reorganize schools yet teachers can still remain as they were. You can pull down the walls and make an open school; but open teaching remains an achievement of the teacher's art, and an achievement that is an expression of understanding.

What are the implications of all this for in-service development? My position is that in-service development must be the development of the teacher as artist. That means the development of understanding expressed in performance: understanding of the nature of knowledge expressed in the art form of teaching and learning. No skills unless they enhance understanding. What I am advocating is so radical that I may not be communicating it. Let me sharpen the message in the area of curriculum: I am saying that the purpose of any curriculum change, any curriculum research, any curriculum development is the enhancement of the art of teaching, of understanding expressed as performance. The idea that you want a change and the change is dependent on retraining teachers is a non-starter.

As a starting point teachers must want change, rather than others wanting to change them. That means that the option of professional development leading toward professional satisfaction of a kind that brings an enhancement of self must be made clear and open to teachers. Teachers have been taught that teaching is instrumental. When we say that teaching is an art, we are saying that the craft of teaching is inseparable from the understanding taught. In short, teaching is intrinsic.

Improving education is not about improving teaching as a delivery system. Crucial is the desire of the artist to improve his or her art. This art is what the experienced teacher brings to in-service development. Good in-service education recognizes and strengthens the power and primacy of that art. It offers curricula to teachers as music in-service offers Beethoven or Stravinsky to musicians: to further the art. In-service is linked to curriculum because art is about change and only develops in change. If the art of teaching could develop without change, then there would be no need for change in education. It is art's appetite for change that makes educational change necessary to the virtue of schooling.

The artist is the researcher whose inquiry expresses itself in performance of his or her art rather than (or as well as) in a research report. In an essentially practical art, like education, all the research and all the in-service education we offer should support that research towards performance on the part of the teacher. For there is in education no absolute and unperformed knowledge. In educational research and scholarship the ivory towers where the truth is neglected are so many theatres without players, galleries without pictures, music without musicians. Educational knowledge exists in, and is verified or falsified in, its performance.

## References

CAMPBELL, D.T. and STANLEY, J.C. (1963) 'Experimental and quasi-experimental designs for research on teaching' in GAGE, N.L. (Ed) *Handbook of Research on Teaching* Chicago, Rand McNally.

FIENBERG, S.E. (1977) 'The collection and analysis of ethnographic data in educational research' *Anthropology and Education Quarterly* 8(2) pp. 50–57.

NIXON, J. (Ed) (1981) *A Teacher's Guide to Action Research: Evaluation, Enquiry and Development in the Classroom* London, Grant McIntyre.

STAKE, R.E. and EASLEY, J. (1978) *Case Studies in Science Education Vol. I: The Case Reports. Vol. II: Design, Overview and General Findings* Washington, D.C., Superintendent of Documents, U.S. Government Printing Office. Stock nos. 038–000–00377–1 & 038–000–0037–3.

STENHOUSE, L. (1979) 'Using research means doing research' in DAHL, H., ANDERS, L. and RAND, P. (Eds) *Spotlight on Educational Research* Festschrift to Johannes Sandven. Oslo, Oslo University Press.

STENHOUSE, L. (1980) 'Curriculum research and the art of the teacher' *Curriculum* 1(1) pp. 40–44.

STENHOUSE, L. (1983) *Authority, Education and Emancipation* London, Heinemann.

# Transfer of Training: The Contribution of 'Coaching'

Bruce Joyce and Beverly Showers
San Francisco State University and the
University of Oregon

In an earlier review (Joyce and Showers, 1980), we examined the research on teachers' abilities to acquire teaching skills and strategies. We concluded that, given adequate training conditions, teachers are consistently able both to 'fine-tune' existing skills and learn new ones. Although the data are incomplete with respect to the effects of specific training components (theory/presentation, modelling, practice, feedback) on certain levels of impact (awareness, organized knowledge, skills, application), the literature on training complements that on learning – people learn what they study and practice. Our focus in this chapter is on the transfer of acquired or mastered skills to classroom practice. As trainers, how do we facilitate and support the eventual goal of learning – the use of knowledge and skill in unique settings?

Trainers have often operated as though their task was completed with the achievement of skill mastery. The assumption that teachers (or any learners) will automatically transfer their learning to new settings is not, however, strongly supported by the research on training. We have to consider not only how to help teachers acquire and improve their skills but also how to help them integrate those skills into their active repertoire. Research on the implementation of innovations appears to indicate that transfer of skills may be a far more complex stage of learning than has been generally recognized.

## Implementation of Innovations

The period from the late 1950s to the early 1970s saw the introduction of a great number of innovations in the organization of schools and in school staffs (largely various forms of 'differentiated staffing' or 'team teaching'), specific curriculums (the 'new' science and mathematics, alternative approaches to Social Studies, etc.) and general approaches to school (e.g., the open classroom). By the end of that period it had become apparent that the degree of implementation of these had varied quite widely and that even the well implemented instances of innovation had been eroded by time (see Goodlad and Klein, 1970; Weiss, 1978; Berman and McLaughlin, 1978). Informal observations, surveys, and formal evaluations of curriculums have produced findings generally congruent with the above assertions. That is, there is great variability, even within sites, with respect to the implementation of curriculum and that even well implemented curricular and organizational changes tend to disappear fairly rapidly.

What is of concern here is to determine whether there are parallels in the curriculum implementation literature and the training literature. In both cases we have a problem that the literature is uneven and that relatively few studies permit us to make firm inferences about the relationship between the strategies that are employed and the degree of use, especially over the long term. Fullan and Pomfret (1977) identified dimensions of implementation: understanding of the rationale of a curriculum; the use of appropriate materials and instructional processes; appropriate changes between the role relationships of teachers and students; and appropriate evaluation – and suggested that the degree to which these dimensions are used varies considerably. They observed, in fact, that the utilization of instructional materials is more likely to occur than a change in instructional process, pupil/teacher role relationships, or evaluation.

Notwithstanding the difficulties, we have attempted to determine the degree of match between the working hypotheses we have generated in the training literature and the better studies in curriculum implementation. Looking at the studies by Gross *et al* (1971); Charters and Pellegrin (1973); Crowther (1972); Downey (1975); Lukas and Wohlleb (1973) and Nauman-Etienne (1974), Fullan and Pomfret suggest that the less explicit the characteristics and rationale of the innovation, the more likely there will be user confusion and frustration and a low degree of implementation. This is similar to our contention that an understanding of the theory of an approach to teaching contributes to the development of skill and ultimately to its use. In both cases what it seems to boil down to is the common-sense proposition that the more thoroughly one understands something the more likely one is to be able to learn how to use it and be committed to using it.

Second, although Fullan and Pomfret do not discriminate between various aspects of training, they have examined the inclusion of in-service training as a factor in bringing about degrees of implementation. Elements of training have not been explicitly studied in curriculum applications but most of the researchers have concluded that intensive 'in-service training (as distinct from single workshops or pre-service training) is an important strategy for implementation' (p. 373).

Some of the reports are quite instructive. Downey (1975) reported a low degree of implementation in a well-thought-out and rationalized social studies curriculum in the Province of Alberta, Canada. The in-service work was in most cases a 'theory-only' treatment; that is, in short workshops the rationale was discussed and materials were distributed, but practice, feedback and coaching were virtually absent. From the training literature alone we would have predicted that the implementation effort would have failed in much the way Downey found that it did.

On the other hand, in the implementation of the planned variation of Head Start (Lukas and Wohlleb, 1973) fairly high degrees of implementation were evident in many sites where the developers worked directly explaining the rationale, providing materials, demonstrating, providing coaching and moral support.

Similarly, evaluation of the Humanities Curriculum Project in England (Hamingson, 1973; and McDonald and Walker, 1974) compared a sample of schools in which the teachers received training by the sponsors of innovation and one in which the materials had been brought together but in which there was no direct training. In the first sample, the training provided was fairly substantial and included many elements which we have identified in the training literature. Not only was implementation much greater for the trained group but pupil achievement scores shifted much more in those schools where the teachers had been trained. Thus not only was there greater implementation but the implementation resulted in pupil learning changes in the desired direction.

The curriculum literature also provides support for the notion that the provision of materials and both coaching and psychological support from consultants are important contributors to implementation. Although the evidence is by no means firm, the analysts of the curriculum implementation literature recommend that demonstration lessons be provided, that opportunity to learn skills be included, that coaching for both skill development and psychological support be provided, and also that materials, at least sample units and preferably adequate materials to support the implementation, be provided, explained and demonstrated. The curriculum implementation litera- ture has tended to cite of either very weak treatments (theory-only or theory-plus-materials-only), or evidence of a massive inservice effort which, while not explicitly identifying the elements which have emerged from the training literature, appears to include all or most of them. In the former case, little implementation occurs on the part of most teachers, while in the latter case, relatively high degrees of implementation are reported.

The curriculum literature thus adds the provision of resources to the paradigm if one wishes a high degree of implementation to occur. It also directs our attention towards the organizational variables and the macro-socio-political variables of schools and schooling that are unquestionably important but out of the scope of our specific concern here.

To this the National Science Foundation Studies (Stake and Easley, 1978) add a number of other elements. The provision of subject matter information and how to apply it explicitly to a new curriculum is cited frequently, implying an expansion of the theory component in training systems. The results of those investigations also emphasize the provision of materials, affirm the amounts of relearning necessary if new teaching methods are to be acquired and utilized, and affirm also the need for consultants who can provide coaching during the implementation period.

Thus the overall impression is that there is a relatively high degree of congruence between the curriculum implementation litera- ture and the literature on training. In addition, attention needs to be focused on factors having to do with the materials and the importance of a favourable macro-social context and organizational climate at the particular school sites.

Finally, demands for accountability and for demonstration of effective training programmes have prompted calls for studies of transfer (Wilen and Kindsvatter, 1978; Timm, 1975; Laktasic, 1976). Documentation of skill loss, where follow-up is done, has reempha- sized the fact that we cannot assume transfer after skills are acquired.

Given the disappointing history of educational innovations, and the role in-service education is believed to play in implementation, we have hypothesized that the integration of new skills and strategies into classroom practice will require the additional training compo- nent 'coaching'. It is probable that classroom application of teaching skills and strategies represents a transfer task for both teachers and trainers.

## Transfer of Training

In the literature from psychology, transfer usually refers to 'the influence of prior learning upon later learning' (Klausmeier and Davis, 1969) and the distinction is made between lateral and vertical transfer. Transfer is lateral when a person generalizes learning to a new task of the same complexity. An example in teaching occurs when a science teacher, having learned to use advance organizers to structure lectures and readings in chemistry, applies the same techniques to structure lectures and readings in physics. Vertical, or cumulative transfer is the condition in which 'knowledge and abilities acquired in performing one task facilitates the learning of higher-order tasks' (Klausmeier and Davis, 1969, p. 1483). An example in teaching occurs when a science teacher who has taken a chemistry course using inductive laboratory exercises, organizes and teaches a course built around inductive laboratory experiences. The skills learned as a student are elevated to the teaching function – a more complex application requiring judgment and management not required in the student role. Essentially transfer can be positive or negative, depending on whether prior learning facilitates or retards future learning, or there can be zero transfer, as when prior learning has no effect on later learning. A primary goal of teachers and teacher educators is positive, cumulative transfer of learning as teaching skills learned in the training setting are applied in the school.

The study of transfer has typically followed a research paradigm in which an experimental group receives training and both the experimental and control group are then tested on a transfer task that is dissimilar in some way to the training task. Posttests for transfer generally follow training by several weeks or months. In contrast, studies of training, which also frequently employ a treatment and control group, seldom check for skill fidelity in applied settings following training. (There are exceptions, of course, e.g., Johnson and Sloat, 1980; Perkins and Atkinson, 1973; Moore and Schaut, 1979.)

The positive, cumulative transfer of learned teaching skills and strategies to classroom practice is enormously complex. Newly acquired skills must be integrated into an existing repertoire of skills and knowledge. Curriculums must be reexamined for appropriate uses of new skills, and goals must be reviewed in relation to new strategies. Thus, learning to perform a new skill or strategy is only the first step toward affecting student outcomes. Transfer of training to the learning environment requires skilful decision making by the classroom teacher and redirection of behaviour until the new skill is operating comfortably within the flow of activities in the classroom.

A well documented example of the difficulty of integrating a new skill can be found in the research on 'higher-order' questioning skills. Teachers learned to discriminate higher-order from lower-order questions, to generate examples of each, and to increase their rate of higher-order questions in both micro-teaching and regular classroom environments. Does this indicate a successful training programme? Yes and no. Teachers definitely acquired new knowledge and facility and demonstrated them in teaching situations. However, subsequent research indicated student learning decrements for greater rates of higher order questions. Apparently, teacher use of higher order questions results in greater student gains only in very specific situations (for example, when a foundation of facts is first established). The presumption is that the skill as such was learned (the ability to ask higher order questions) but that in the process of transfer the additional and more complex skills involved in selecting and using higher order questions appropriately were not developed. Vertical transfer did not occur where it was needed.

Ellis (1965:72–74), after reviewing research on transfer of learning summarized some major principles which are significant when we consider the transfer of skills to classroom practice.

1 *Overall task similarity*
   Transfer of training is greatest when the training conditions are highly similar to those of the ultimate testing conditions.

This finding suggests that training conditions that approximate the interactive classroom teaching situation are most likely to facilitate transfer. Thus we would expect greater transfer of teaching skills when in-service programs include opportunities to practice skills in peer teaching, micro-teaching, and simulations, and less transfer for training when only theory or rationales, presentation of materials and demonstration or modelling.

2 *Practice and Transfer*
   a *Learning to learn.* Cumulative practice in learning a series of related tasks of problems leads to increased facility in learning how to learn. Joyce and his associates (1981) have demonstrated the applicability of this principle in their

studies of teachers' ability to acquire models of teaching (1980) which are new to them. Teachers who have mastered two or more new models apparently learn further new models with greater ease than the first ones they study.

b *Early-task learning.* Transfer is maximized if greater effort is spent in mastering the early ones of a series of tasks. Weil's results (Joyce *et al* 1981) support this principle in teacher training. She found that the prior mastery of 'model relevant' skills facilitates the acquisition of specific teaching models.

c *Amount of practice on the original task.* The greater the amount of practice on the original task, the greater the likelihood of positive transfer; negative transfer is likely to occur following only limited practice on the original task. Our estimate is that very few teacher training programmes provide anything like the amount of practice necessary to apply new skills in the classroom. (Our current estimate is that a teacher needs to practice a model of teaching from ten to twenty times in simulated conditions before there can be a reasonable expectation to transfer.)

These transfer principles all refer to optimal amounts of practice for achieving transfer, and as such, provide useful guidelines for the design of training as well as possible explanations for the failure of much of our training to transfer to classroom practice. We can predict from these principles that successful training programmes will have to teach original tasks thoroughly and provide multiple opportunities for practice – many more than are commonly provided in preservice or inservice programs.

3 *Task or stimulus variety.*
In general, variety of tasks, or of their stimulus components, during original learning increases the amount of positive transfer obtained.

Teachers learning new skills need opportunities to observe multiple uses and applications of the new behaviours. This suggests numerous demonstrations of new strategies for different subject areas and grade levels. As teachers begin to understand the adaptation of a strategy in the training situation, probabilities for classroom adaptation increase.

4 *Understanding and transfer.*
Transfer is greater if the learner understands the general rules or principles which are appropriate in solving new problems.

This principle supports the thorough presentation of the theory and rationale underlying specific teaching skills and strategies. It is possible that much of the teacher criticism of in-service education as 'too theoretical' results from either theory only treatments or incomplete presentations of theory. When underlying principles are incompletely developed, they provide no basis for action and are indeed of little use.

Should we assume however, that more adequate theory, demonstration and practice will, by themselves, assure transfer? We believe not, given the difficulty of integrating new (and therefore difficult and awkward) behaviours into an existing and often quite comfortable routine. For most people to use an innovation to the extent that it becomes coherent in the context of their existing teaching style probably requires the companionship, support and instruction provided by what we call on-site coaching.

### Coaching

Coaching is characterized by an observation and feedback cycle in an ongoing instructional or clinical situation. Although self-coaching is possible, coaching usually involves a collegial approach to the analysis of teaching for the purpose of integrating mastered skills and strategies into: a) a curriculum; b) a set of instructional goals; c) a time span; and d) a personal teaching style.

As a training device, coaching differs from training for skill acquisition on several dimensions. Practice remains important, as unused skills tend to atrophy. Feedback, however, rather than emphasizing fidelity to a skill or model, stresses the appropriateness of specific strategies to certain goals, Together, the teacher and 'coach' examine appropriate places in the curriculum for the use of specific strategies, evaluate the effectiveness of observed lessons, and plan for future trials. This phase of training represents a continuing problem-solving endeavour between the teacher and the 'coach'. The purpose of this instruction is to ensure vertical transfer – to increase the probability that application will take place. We believe that a major problem in teacher training designs has been the assumption that a skill, once learned, can be 'popped into place' in the classroom (that is, transferred laterally). The situation is, rather, that transfer of teaching skill involves much new learning – when to use the skills, how to modulate them to the students, etc. – this learning has to take place in the process of transfer.

Clearly, coaching is a labour-intensive approach to training. In-service education budgets, which seldom provide for more than two or three school or district-wide programmes during a school year, are unlikely to expand suddenly to provide centralized resources for coaching. A realignment of the resources committed to in-service education, however, could accomplish substantial increases in coaching. Training systems aimed at developing coaching skills for teachers and principals would create cadres of trained coaches at school sites.

The implementation record for educational innovations, the study of effective training, and the research on transfer support the notion of more intensive in-service training. The tendency of even well-learned skills to dissipate in classroom situations supports the concept of coaching as a training device, and the training research provides a promising model for the teaching of 'coaching' skills.

Research on training that investigates the relationship of coaching to transfer of learning is needed. If coaching should significantly boost the rate of implementation of new skills, strategies, and curriculum for long periods of time, it will be possible to measure much more meaningfully the effects of specific innovations on student learning.

In the meantime, we should operate on the best knowledge we have. In our opinion that means:

The use of the integrated theory-demonstration-practice-feedback training programmes to ensure skill development.

The use of considerable amounts of practice in simulated conditions to ensure fluid control of the new skills.

The employment of regular on-site coaching to facilitate vertical transfer – the development of new learning in the process of transfer.

The preparation of teachers who can provide one another with the needed coaching.

## References

BERMAN, P. and McLAUGHLIN, M.W. (1978) *Federal Programs Supporting Educational Change. Vol. VIII: Implementing and Sustaining Innovations* Santa Monica, CA, Rand.

CHARTERS, W.W. and PELLEGRIN, R. (1973) 'Barriers to the innovation process: Four case studies of differentiated staffing' *Administrative*

*Science Quarterly* 1, pp. 3–14.

CROWTHER, F. (1972) Factors Affecting the Rate of Adoption of the 1971 Alberta Social Studies Curriculum for Elementary Schools. Master's Thesis, University of Alberta.

DOWNEY, L. and ASSOCIATES (1975) *The Social Studies in Alberta* Edmonton, Alberta, L. Downey Research Associates.

ELLIS, H. (1965) *The Transfer of Learning* New York, Macmillan.

FULLAN, M. and POMFRET, A. (1977) 'Research on curriculum and instruction implementation' *Review of Educational Research* 47, pp. 335–397.

GOODLAD, J. and KLEIN, F. (1970) *Looking Behing the Classroom Door* Worthington, Ohio, Charles E. Jones.

GROSS, N., GIACQUINTA, F. and BERSTEIN, M. (1971) *Implementing Organizational Innovation: A Sociological Analysis of Planned Educational Change* New York, Basic Books.

HAMINGSON, D. (Ed) (1973) *Toward Judgement* Norwich, UK, University of East Anglia. (The publication of the Evaluation Unit of the Humanities Curriculum Project, 1970–72).

JOHNSON, J. and SLOAT, K.C. (1980) 'Teacher training effects: Real or illusory' *Psychology in the Schools* 17, pp. 109–115.

JOYCE, B.R. and SHOWERS, B.K. (1980) 'Improving in-service training: The message of research' *Educational Leadership* 37, pp. 379–385.

JOYCE, B. and WEIL, M. (1980) *Models of Teaching* (2nd ed) Englewood Cliffs, NJ, Prentice Hall.

JOYCE, B., BROWN, C. and PECK, L. (1981) *Flexibility in Teaching* New York, Longman.

KLAUSMEIER, H.J. and DAVIS, J.K. (1969) 'Transfer of learning' in EBEL, R.L. (Ed) *Encyclopedia of Educational Research* (4th ed) Toronto, Ontario, Macmillan.

LAKTASIC, S. (1976) 'Achieving transfer of learning through simulation' ERIC No. ED 150 144,

LUKAS, C. and WOHLLEB, C. (1973) *Implementation on Head Start Planned Variation: 1970–71, Part 1 & 2* Cambridge, Mass, Huron Institute.

MCDONALD, B. and WALKER, R. (Eds) (1974) *Innovation Evaluation, Research and the Problem of Control* Norwich, UK, SAFARI Project, University of East Anglia.

MOORE, J.W. and SCHAUT, J.A. (1979) 'Increasing instructional effectiveness through the use of a problem-solving approach to the design of instructional systems' *Journal of Experimental Education* 47, pp. 156–161.

NAUMANN-ETIENNE, M. (1974) Bringing About Open Education: Strategies for Innovation. Unpublished doctoral dissertation, University of Michigan.

PERKINS, S.R. and ATKINSON, D.R. (1973) 'Effects of selected techniques for training assistants in human relations skills' *Journal of Counselling Psychology* 20, pp. 84–90.

STAKE, R.E. and EASLEY, J. (1978) *Case Studies in Science Education Vol I, The Case Reports Vol II Design, Overview and General Findings* Washington DC, Superintendent of Documents US Government Printing Office: Stock Nos 038–000–00377–1 and 038–000–0037–3.

TIMM, A.E. (1975) An Analysis of Classroom Teachers' Translation of the Ideas Gained from In-service Experience into Classroom Procedures. Unpublished doctoral dissertation, University of Pittsburgh.

WEISS, I.B. (1978) *National Survey of Science, Mathematics, and Social Studies Education* Washington, DC, United States Government Printing Office.

WILEN, W.W. and KINDSVATTER, R. (1978) 'Implications for effective in-service education' *The Clearing House* 51, pp. 391–396.

# The Principal as an Agent of Knowledge Utilization (KU) for School Improvement*

## Michael Fullan
### Ontario Institute for Studies in Education

After twenty years of meaningless generalities, such as the principal is the gatekeeper of change, researchers are finally beginning to define and study exactly what the role of the principal is and might be regarding change in schools. Fortunately, there is some very good detailed research currently ongoing on the role of the principal vis-a-vis change. While systematic research is not yet available, we do have some good beginnings. I review this work in three parts: first, large scale surveys on the role of the principal; second, focused research findings on the role of the principal in facilitating or inhibiting change and KU of teachers; and third, conclusions about the role of principals as KU's and as agents of KU.

### Large Scale Surveys

There have been recent national or state surveys of the role of elementary school principals (Pharis and Zakariya, 1979) and secondary school principals (Abramowitz and Tenebaum, 1978, Byrne *et al*, 1978 and Gorton and McIntyre 1978) in the United States, and principals from across all levels in the province of Ontario, Canada (Eastabrook and Fullan, 1978). These studies provide a broad context for considering the role of the principal.

In the Pharis and Zakariya (1979:28) study the most frequent 'source of ideas for recent innovation' for elementary school principals were 'other principals and teachers' (23% named this category in a mutually exclusive rating). However, professional reading (19%) and

* This chapter appears in expanded form in LEHMING, R. and KANE, M. (Eds) (1981) *Improving Schools*, Beverly Hills, California, Sage.

local workshops (16%) were frequently used by substantial numbers of principals as the percentage indicates. In rating the value of certain types of preparation for the job, 85% named on the job experience as a teacher and principal as having 'much value', while only 36% mentioned graduate education, and 24% in-service programmes. Since in-service programmes for principals are becoming more widespread, some attention must be paid to what constitutes useful and less than useful in-service programmes. (See Fullan 1979 and Reinhard *et al*, 1980).

Orlich and his colleagues have examined the role of principals in innovation in Washington State. In a survey of 100 school principals concerning the use of social science innovation, Ruff and Orlich (1974: 390) found that textbook salesmen were listed by principals as the best source of information (53%), followed by the district curriculum director (40%); no other source was listed by more than 7%. In a later study of social science and science curriculum innovation, Orlich *et al* (1976) found similar results. For social science, 50% of the principals mentioned commercial publishers as the best source, 43% cited district curriculum coordinators, and 33% mentioned books, journals, etc. Similar results were found regarding science innovations. One further finding directly related to the purpose of the survey was that principals who had attended National Science Foundation workshops (about one half the sample) were much more likely to list workshops as significant sources of ideas for innovation than were non-NSF principals. Thus, focused workshops can be useful, but are not frequently utilized.

In a study of the senior high school principalship, Byrne *et al*, (1978:6) found that principals do report a high level of involvement in conferences and workships – 79% said that they attended workshops and conferences within the district, and 62% outside the district. The relationship to KU is unknown, but one might suspect that the effectiveness of workshops has not been great given what we know about problems of conducting effective in-service.

When senior principals were asked to rate how essential certain types of pre-service courses were, it is interesting to compare the 1965 and 1977 findings summarized below:

Two findings are worth highlighting for our purposes. First, the overall amount and range of essential knowledge as seen by principals has increased dramatically; 5 of the 6 categories show major increases reflecting what some principals see as the problems of role overload and the need for role clarification in the contemporary principalship. Second, curriculum development, which is closest to our concern

| Course | *1977*<br>*% Rated Essential* | *1965*<br>*% Rated Essential* |
|---|---|---|
| School Law | 77 | 32 |
| Curriculum and Programme Development | 76 | 41 |
| School Management | 74 | 26 |
| Supervision of Instruction | 71 | 56 |
| Human Relations | 71 | 45 |
| Administrative Theory and Practice | 32 | 41 |

*Source:* Byrne *et al*, 1978:10

with KU for school improvement, shows a major increase from two-fifths of the principals who said it was essential in 1965 to three-quarters in 1977. Even more interesting is the rank ordering of how principals 'do spend time' compared to how they think they 'should spend time.' Programme development was ranked 5 out of 9 tasks in terms of 'do' and 1 out of 9 in terms of 'should'.

In a subsample of the sixty most 'effective' principals (identified through reputational criteria), Gorton and McIntyre (1978) found that these so-called effective principals focused more on programme development than the sample as a whole. In time actually spent, programme development was ranked 1 of 9 in time spent during the previous two weeks, and 3 of 9 in time spent over the whole year (compared to 5 of 9 for the larger sample). However, teacher perceptions of these principals was different. Teachers indicated an actual rank order of 5, and a 'should' rank order of 1 (we cannot compare this with the larger sample, because teachers were not sampled). Principal's role in curriculum change varied from school to school (Gordon and McIntyre, 1978:22):

> a few principals indicated that they initiate ideas, often subtly through others, but more typically the principals view themselves as catalysts, facilitators, reviewers, and resource providers.

Principals listed teachers, individually or by departments, as the primary initiators of curriculum changes, and themselves as the initiators of or facilitators of major changes in the school. The authors of the study formulate a composite of the change strategy used by the sixty principals: 1) recognize the need and plant the seed with staff members and/or others; 2) work with people, especially those most affected – but do not impose change; 3) provide needed resources and support (Gorton and McIntyre, 1978:61). The sample of exemplary principals cited 'role clarification' as the number one need, and that excessive paper work and district meetings were a major drain on their time.

The exemplary principals are by definition not representative of principals as a whole. In more general surveys, the prominence of the principal on KU decisions is minimal. This is not to say that principals are unimportant. Indeed, their lack of prominence in KU may be one of the main causes of lack of implementation or KU of teachers. Aoki *et al* (1977) found that principals were rarely mentioned by a large sample of social studies teachers as 'sources of information'. Barrows (1980) investigated the adoption decisions in thirteen sites which were using Individually Guided Education. Not only were principals involved in decisions to adopt the innovation in only two of the thirteen cases, there were only three cases in which principals had the 'opportunity to confirm the adoption decisions' (that is, the central office made the decision in ten of the thirteen schools). Havelock and Havelock's (1973) national survey of superintendents also found that principals were rarely mentioned as key factors in adopted innovations.

Generally, similar findings on time spent are reported by Eastabrook and Fullan (1978) in their Ontario sample – 44% of the principals said that they actually spend a great deal of time on curricular tasks, while 76% indicated that they would ideally like to spend a great deal of time on such tasks. The percentages were reversed for administrative tasks (paper work, meetings, etc.).

The above findings provide a general context for considering the role of the principal. Among the findings and gaps are the following:

1    Principals probably are exposed to more ideas than are teachers. However, only a minority find workshops, reading, etc. as valuable. Other principals and teachers are the preferred source, but this too, is in the minority.

2    Both elementary and secondary principals say that they would like to spend more time on programme improvement than they do. The veracity of this statement must be examined, since this represents a socially desirable response.

3    The overload of responsibilities in school management, administrative requirements, public relations etc. interferes

with principal involvement in KU, and makes prioritizing of activities difficult.

4   Effective principals play a direct or facilitative role in KU and school improvement, but it is not at all clear what this means in practice (see the next section).

5   The general findings do not indicate major differences between elementary and secondary school principals, but surely there are important differences according to size and level of schooling. One would expect that principals in large secondary schools would perform more of an administrative and indirect role, but the study of sixty effective senior high school principals indicated that they actively support curriculum improvement.

## Research Findings on the Principal and KU

Up until 1975 there were very few empirical studies on what the principal does and does not do in relation to educational change (there is still only a small number of studies, although it is increasing rapidly). Wolcott's (1973) ethnography is rich in detail, but is based on a sample of one. Wolcott reports that Ed's (the principal) formal preparation for the role of the principal was 'simply a fact of life that he had to take courses' (p. 178), and that his courses were of little or no help to his work. Similarly, in-service work was done mainly to meet district requirements ('I have been involved in workshops "up to here",' p. 199). As to KU from research sources, Ed had a number of journals and books on his shelf, but, observes Wolcott, 'I know of no occasion when Ed so much as glanced toward any of the materials on the shelf' (p. 200). Ironically, research was cited to support certain decisions – Ed often resorted to an answer frequently employed by other principals as well: 'I think you will find that studies have shown . . .' (p. 205). Wolcott, as many others have found, adds that principals and teachers rarely interact on professional matters except to do what is minimally required for teacher evaluation. Sarason (1971) states that many principals handle the dilemma of interacting with teachers by minimizing interaction. Both sides, in effect, agree to leave each other alone.

Wolcott (1973:307) also suggests that principals work more to manage change introduced from outside than to lead change:

Principals talk a great deal about change. But I did not see any evidence that Ed actually contributed to this movement. The school principal is successful in his work to the extent that he is able to contain and constrain the forces of change with which he must contend as a matter of daily routine.

The principal according to Wolcott is interested in maintaining an image of change, but is more prudent in dealing with the real thing. In any case, the history of the role of the principal in educational change is not compelling. Sarason (1971, 115) states quite boldly:

There is little in the nature of the classroom teacher, there is little in the motivation of the teacher to become a principal, there is little in the actual experience of the teacher with principals, and there is even less in the criteria by which a principal is chosen to expect that the role of the principal will be viewed as a vehicle, and in practice used, for educational change and innovation.

Recent empirical evidence confirms that the majority of principals play a limited role in educational change. Crowson and Porter-Gehrie (1980) recently reported findings from an intensive observation study of twenty-six urban school principals. The overwhelming emphasis and pressure in their daily work was toward stability and maintenance, specifically 1) maintaining student disciplinary control, 2) keeping outside influences under control and building external support, 3) keeping staff conflicts at bay, and 4) keeping the school supplied with adequate resources. It is revealing to note that Crowson and Porter-Gehrie's 'natural' description of what principals do rarely mentions KU behaviour aside from some aspects of 'keeping the school supplied with adequate resources' (even the latter referred primarily to basic supplies and staff rather than KU).

In a larger scale study directly involving innovative projects, Berman and McLaughlin (1977:131) report that one-third of the teachers in their study thought that their principal functioned primarily as an administrator. Teachers rated these principals as ineffective and uninvolved in change. Berman and McLaughlin do not say how many of the other two-thirds were actively engaged in change (moreover, their sample was based on school districts which adopted innovative projects). The authors do, however, indicate what successful principals did. They found that 'projects having the active support of the principal were the most likely to fare well' (Berman and McLaughlin, 1977:124). They claim that principals' actions serve to legitimate whether a change is to be taken seriously, and serve to support teachers. They also note that one of the best indicators of active involvement is whether the principal attended workshop sessions with their teachers.

Emrick and Peterson's (1978) synthesis of five major studies, and the work of Hall and Loucks at Texas confirm that KU is unlikely to occur in the absence of direct administrative support, especially by principals. Cases of effective involvement by principals are cited, and indicated as in the minority. Loucks and Hall (1979:18) describe an effective elementary school principal who was instrumental in bringing about KU of a new science program:

> In this school the teachers knew that teaching the science programme was a priority, the principal makes certain that new teachers and those at new grade levels receive the necessary training to teach the new units ... He constantly visited classrooms, assisted with lessons, and talked about children continually.

Levels of implementation at this school were higher than in other schools where most principals gave at best a general endorsement of the programme, and indicated that use of it was up to the teacher. In a more recent paper Hall *et al* (1980) examined nine schools more closely using a case study methodology and were very explicit about the implications of their results (p. 26):

> For us, the single most important hypothesis emanating from these data is that the degree of implementation of the innovation is different in different schools because of the actions and concerns of the principal. At this time it appears that a most important factor to explain the quality and quantity of change in these schools is the concerns of the principals and what the principals did and did not do.

It seems, then, that the principal's interest in instruction is of critical importance (at least at the elementary school level). Corroborating this is Wellisch *et al*'s (1978) in-depth study of twenty-two elementary schools in which they related 'principal's leadership in instruction' to 'school success in raising reading and maths achievement of students'. The sample was part of a national evaluation of school districts supported through the Emergency School Aid Act (ESAA). Teachers and principals were asked if the principal felt strongly about instruction, had definite ideas, and promoted a point of view (p. 215). They found that 'schools where principals felt strongly about instruction were significantly more likely to show gains in achievement' (p. 216). Owens and Steinhoff (1976:152) describe an identical finding in which two matched urban schools were compared (matched on basic characteristics except that one school consistently out-performed the other in reading achievement tests). The only discernible difference between the two schools was 'the leader behaviour of the two principals' in which one principal played a direct role in instructional planning and the other did not.

Despite the appearance of many commonalities in the above studies (see also Lipham 1980), we still know very little about the proportion of principals who may be engaged in KU efforts. Even more problematic is the lack of conceptualization and specification of different roles played by different principals within the domain of change. Stated another way, different change directed behaviours may be more or less effective either in their own right, or under different conditions. These issues are addressed in the rest of this section.

Variations in the role of principals have been examined by several other researchers. Hyde (1977) analyzed the problem-solving methods of nine principals in the Documentation and Technical Assistance project. Seven of the nine principals 'managed' their problems in essentially an administrative manner (bureaucratic paperwork, announcements, etc.), four placed a major emphasis on educational interaction (curriculum, teaching, etc.), and four worked as coordinating managers (coordinating assistant principals, department chairpersons, etc.). We can note for future reference that three of the four principals with educational interaction approaches were elementary school principals, and three of the four coordinating managers were at the high school level. Administrative preoccupation occurred equally at both levels.

Leithwood *et al* (1978) observed and interviewed twenty-seven principals from three school districts. They discovered four types of leaders – administrative (50%), facilitative (31%), directive (12%) and interpersonally oriented (8%). In other words, when it came to curriculum change, one-half of the sample operated basically as administrators. In the words of the authors (Leithwood *et al.* 1978:66):

> The administrative leader is essentially a passive observer of the curriculum process in his school. He keeps track of what is going on and may make suggestions on an infrequent basis, he becomes directly involved only if there is a visible problem.

Equally interesting is the distinction between facilitative and directive leaders, because both play an instructional change leadership role. The facilitative leaders were 'highly involved in the curriculum decisions of teachers' (p. 70). They used a variety of strategies to organize and influence teachers. They established priorities, but 'relied heavily upon teachers to influence other teachers' (p. 71). By contrast, the more directive leaders decided themselves on the nature of change, and attempted to get their teachers to follow their decisions. The distinction is important, because research on the principal which lumps together all principals who are involved in change may result in misleading or inconsistent findings. For example, in Miles' (1978) case study of two open space schools, one principal actively intervened in the implementation process, while the other didn't (pp. 113, 127). As it turned out, it was the non-active principal who had the most influence on later implementation. This seems puzzling until we realize that it is the quality of activity and its relationship to the whole set of factors we have been discussing that is important. Thus, active involvement and support of the principal is important for KU, but not in the form of direct imposition or naive endorsement of change. More generally, the complexities of the meaning of principal support for an innovation are considerable. We need more research which describes the different change roles played by principals because there are conflicting findings about how directive principals are or should be in change efforts and with what consequences.

It is no theoretical and empirical accident, one would hope, that Margaret Thomas (1978) identified essentially the same three roles as did Leithwood *et al* in her study of principals in the alternative school programmes in Alum Rock, California; Minneapolis, Minnesota; Cincinnati, Ohio; and Eugene, Oregon. Thomas (1978:12–13) describes the three roles:

> *The Director* – this principal makes the decisions in his school, both procedural and substantive. He will take a great interest in things affecting the classroom, such as curriculum, teaching techniques, and staff development and training, as well as those things affecting the school as a whole, such as scheduling and budgeting. Teachers in a school with this type of principal contribute to decisions affecting the classroom, but the principal retains final decision-making authority.

> *The Administrator* – this principal tends to separate procedural decisions from substantive decisions. He will give teachers

a large measure of autonomy in their own classrooms – over what they teach and how they teach – but will tend to make the decisions in areas that affect the school as a whole. He will perceive his functions as distinct from those of his faculty, and will tend to identify with district management rather than with his staff.

*Facilitator* – this principal perceives his role as one of support; his primary function will be to assist teachers in the performance of their duties. Unlike the administrator, however, this principal will be more concerned with process than with procedures. Principals who exhibit this type of behaviour often perceive themselves as colleagues of their faculty, and are most apt to involve their teachers in the decision-making process.

We cannot entertain a detailed analysis of the four school districts, but the aggregate figures can be reported for the total sixty-eight schools across the four districts.

| *Perceived Prinicpal Behaviour Type* | N | % |
|---|---|---|
| Director | 18 | 26.5 |
| Administrator | 33 | 48.5 |
| Facilitator | 17 | 25.0 |
| | 68 | 100.0 |

(compiled from Thomas, 1978)

Again, this is not a representative sample, and Thomas' definition of director is perhaps more comprehensive than Leithwood's. In any case, the percentage of administratively oriented principals (as perceived by teachers) is virtually the same in the two studies – half the sample.

In attempting to describe the nature of different change related roles of principals, we are helped in a perverse way (the problem becomes more complex) by Blumberg and Greenfield's (1980) study of the effective principal. The authors sought out recommendations of the most effective principal, and selected eight principals to represent diversity (elementary/secondary, rural/urban, male/female). All eight principals were very effective in their schools, but were quite different in their predominant approaches to their work.

Blumberg and Greenfield describe the eight principals with eight different labels – the problem solver, the value-based juggler, the authentic helper, the broker, the humanist, the catalyst, the rationalist, and the politician. There were some common basic elements to their approaches. Blumberg and Greenfield (1980:208) describe three – vision, initiative and resources:

> Their individual commitment to the realization of a particular educational or organizational vision;
>
> Their propensity to assume the initiative and to take a proactive stance to the demands of their work environment;
>
> Their ability to satisfy the routine organizational maintenance demands in a manner that permits them to spend most of their on-the-job time in activities directly related to the realization of their personal vision. They do not allow themselves to become consumed by second-order priorities.

The latter comment is particularly revealing in light of the frequent finding that many principals are preoccupied with administrative details and routine.

The eight principals could not articulate conceptually what they did, but Blumberg and Greenfield (1980:257) summarize the principals' orientation to KU:

> all of them were very skilled at analyzing and determining the requirements of their school situations, and indicating alternative courses of action. This was, like their disposition to collect information as they moved through their work world, a continuous process. They were constantly sorting, sifting, categorizing, and interrelating phenomena bearing on the principalship.

A further relevant finding was the almost complete absence of interaction with fellow principals despite the desire to do so (Blumberg and Greenfield, 1980:168), nor was there a great deal of interaction with superiors. The words Blumberg and Greenfield most frequently use to describe the relationship of principals to those outside their school is isolation and loneliness.

Perhaps, most significant to KU is the finding that at the time of writing the results, seven of the eight principals had either left their positions or were planning to leave (either to promotion or alternative lines of work). Lipham (1980, 212) also found that the departure of the principal was the most important reason 'for a school's abandoning an educational innovation' – echoes of Louis' (1981) recent findings in the R & D Utilization Project.

## Conclusions About the Role of the Principal in KU

There is a mess of variables which must be sorted out before we can understand the apparent inconsistencies and details of the KU behaviour of principals. We might best summarize the research in three parts – what do we know about principals as users of knowledge, what do we know about them as agents of KU for teachers, and what are the most important research gaps we should identify.

### *Principals as Knowledge Users*

Principals on a *per capita* basis have more opportunity and access to external sources of knowledge than do teachers. The majority of principals however, do not seem to take advantage of, or the situation does not support them to investigate these sources of information. The most effective principals (by reputation) do draw more extensively on external sources, and name curriculum or instruction as a higher priority. Blumberg and Greenfield also point to the enormous amount of information processing, internal to the school environment which effective principals carry out. Needed research arising from these observations is listed below.

### *Principals as Agents of KU*

Research consistently found that a large percentage of principals (at least one-half) were preoccupied with administrative work and organizational maintenance activities. Of the other principals, the exact role in KU was somewhat ambiguous and variable. There was some evidence that direct leadership in instruction was strongly related to KU (for example, Wellisch *et al*, 1978), but other evidence that it may be dysfunctional (for example, Leithwood *et al*, 1978). By contrast, facilitative leadership by principals was found to be effective (for example, Leithwood *et al*, 1978). These are not necessarily incompatible findings. There are at least three aspects of the problem which need to be clarified. First, we need more operational definitions of directive and facilitative modes. It is likely that different components and meanings are currently being included. For example, directive can range from having a clear instructional image to authoritarian imposition of poorly thought out or centrally directed programmes. Facilitative can range from *laissez-faire* relationship to teachers to one of active support. Second, it is possible (and there was some evidence to support this) that effective elementary school principals play a more direct instructional role and secondary school principals carry out a more indirect role. Third, returning to the multidimensional nature of KU, it may be that centrally derived programmes are more effectively used by directive principals (when they agree with the programme), and individualistic KU is better served by facilitative principals. Despite these variations the research reviewed was clear that some form of active involvement and support by the principal was essential for KU by teachers. Furthermore, these principals had been effective at coping with (delegating, reprioritizing, etc.) administrative processes, which preoccupied their colleagues.

Finally, the research was in agreement that the principal in a positive or negative way is critical – in fact, may be the most critical agent – for KU of teachers.

### Research Gaps

Given that the principal is so important for KU, the research gaps in our knowledge are especially noteworthy.

1 We need research which examines the daily KU behaviour of principals. This research should incorporate internal to the school relationships *vis-à-vis* KU, external to the school relationships *vis-à-vis* KU, formal and informal KU, innovation focused and individual focused KU.

2 We need conceptualization and research on the meaning and main roles of principals (administrative, directive, facilitative, etc.) in relation to KU, including how some principals are able to prioritize or otherwise operate more effectively as KU agents. Research on effective forms of in-service training of principals as managers of change and KU is especially needed (see Reinhard *et al*, 1980, and Blumberg and Greenfield, 1980, Chapter 16).

3 We need research which examines different conditions under which principals work and the consequences for the role of

principals in KU – elementary/secondary differences, rural/urban, school size, centralized/decentralized school districts all should be differentiated in carrying out the research referred to in 1 and 2.

This has been a lengthy review, partly in recognition of the central importance of the principal in KU, and partly because there is a good deal of current research which is worth reporting. The next five years promises to be even more fruitful for describing, understanding and planning for more direct and effective KU roles of principals.

## References

ABRAMOVITZ, S. and TENEBAUM, E. (1978) *High School '77, A Survey of Public Secondary School Principals* Washington, DC, National Institute of Education.

AOKI, E.T., LONGBORD, C., WILLIAMS, D. and WILSON, D. (1977) *British Columbia Social Studies Assessment Vols. 1–3* British Columbia Ministry of Education.

BARROWS, L. (1980) Findings and Implications of the Thirteen School Study. AERA paper.

BERMAN, P. and McLAUGHLIN, M. (1977) *Federal Programs Supporting Educational Change, Vol. VII: Factors Affecting Implementation and Continuation* Santa Monica, CA, Rand.

BLUMBERG, A. and GREENFIELD, W. (1980) *The Effective Principal* Boston, Allyn and Bacon.

BYRNE, D., HINES, S. and McCLEARY, L. (1978) *The Senior High School Principalship* Reston, VA, National Association of Secondary School Principals.

CROWSON, R. and PORTER-GEHRIE, C. (1980) The School Principalship: An Organizational Stability Role. AERA paper.

EASTABROOK, G. and FULLAN, M. (1978) *School and Community: Principals and Community Schools in Ontario* Toronto, Ministry of Education, OISE Press.

EMRICK, J.A. and PETERSON, S.M. (1978) *A Synthesis of Findings Across Five Recent Studies in Educational Dissemination and Change* San Francisco, CA, Far West Laboratory.

FULLAN, M. (1979) *School Focused Inservice Education in Canada* Paris, OECD. Prepared for CERI (Centre for Educational Research and Innovation), OECD Project on Inservice Education for Teachers (INSET).

GORTON, R. and McINTYRE, K. (1978) *The Senior High School Principalship, Vol. II: The Effective Principal* Reston, VA, National Association of Secondary School Principals.

HALL, G., HORD, S. and GRIFFIN, T. (1980) Implementation at the School Building Level: The Development and Analysis of Nine Mini-Case

Studies. AERA paper.

HAVELOCK, R. and HAVELOCK, M. (1973) *Educational Innovation in the United States* Ann Arbor, MI, Institute for Social Research.

HYDE, A. (1977) *Capacities for Solving Problems: Problems and Problem Solving Methods for School Principals* Chicago, Center for New Schools.

LEITHWOOD, K., ROSS, J. and MONTGOMERY, D.J. (1978) *An Empirical Investigation of Teachers' Curriculum Decision-Making Processes and Strategies Used by Curriculum Decision Managers to Influence Such Decision-Making* Toronto, Ontario Institute for Studies in Education.

LIPHAM, J. (1980) 'Change agentry and school improvement: The principal's role' in Northwest Regional Educational Laboratory *Interorganizational Arrangements for Collaborative Efforts: Commissioned Papers* Portland, Oregon, pp. 61–96.

LOUCKS, S. and HALL, E. (1979) Implementing Innovations in Schools: A Concerns-Based approach. AERA paper.

LOUIS, K. (1981) 'The role of external agents in knowledge utilization' in LEHMING, R. and KANE, M. (Eds) *Improving Schools* Beverly Hills, CA, Sage.

MILES, M. (1978) *Westgate Schools: A Case Study of Two Open-Space Elementary Schools Part III* New York, Project on Social Architecture in Education, Center for Policy Research.

MILES, M., SIEBER, S., WILDER, D. and GOLD, B. (1978) *Final Report, Part IV: Conclusions – Reflections on the Case Studies and Implications* New York, Project on Social Architecture in Education, Center for Policy Research.

ORLICH, D., RUFF, T. and HANSEN, H. (1976) 'Stalking curriculum: Or where do principals learn about new programs?' *Educational Leadership* 33, pp. 614–621.

OWENS, R. and STEINHOFF, C. (1976) *Administering Change in Schools* New Jersey, Prentice Hall.

PHARIS, W. and ZAKARIYA, S. (1979) *The Elementary School Principalship in 1978: A Research Study* Arlington, VA, National Association of Elementary School Principals.

REINHARD, D., ARENDS, R., BARNES, M., KETY, W. and WYANT, S. (1980) Great Expectations: The Principal's Role and Inservice Needs in Supporting Change Projects. AERA paper.

RUFF, T. and ORLICH, D. (1974) 'How do elementary school principals learn about curriculum innovations?' *The Elementary School Journal* 74(7) pp. 389–392.

SARASON, S.B. (1971) *The Culture of the School and the Problem of Change* Boston, Allyn and Bacon.

THOMAS, M. (1978) *A Study of Alternatives in American Education, Vol. II:* Santa Monica, CA, Rand.

WELLISH, W.A., MACQUEEN, A.H., CARRIERE, R.A. and DUCK, G.A. (1978) ''School management and organization in successful schools' *Sociology of Education* 51, pp. 211–226.

WOLCOTT, H.F. (1973) *The Man in the Principal's Office* New York, Holt, Rinehard and Winston.

# Section Three:
## Perspectives on Change

The chapters in this section are concerned with different ways of improving schools. **Ted Aoki** presents a critique of the normative approach to curriculum implementation and proposes a view of implementation as praxis; and in so doing he provides a rationale for the alternative approach to school improvement taken in this book. **Ken Eltis** writing from a similar perspective describes ways in which the continuing education of teachers can contribute to school improvement. School based review is an important aspect of school improvement, and in her chapter **Viviane Robinson** analyzes the process – in the context of New Zealand. In the section's final chapter **Philip Runkel** together with **Richard Schmuck** describe organizational development as a change strategy that schools can use (with a little help) to improve themselves. Taken together these chapters provide a introduction to the ways in which school improvement efforts can be carried out.

# Towards a Reconceptualization of Curriculum Implementation

## Ted Aoki
University of Alberta

In this chapter I wish to move towards a fuller understanding of 'curriculum implementation' by exploring two modes of implementation action. To make sense of these modes of implementation, we should situate ourselves in a classroom wherein a teacher and students are in the presence of a curriculum being implemented. For how we view the teacher's implementing action within this situation depends on the perspective used to guide our interpretation of the relationship between the teacher and curriculum. I suggest that such an understanding will help to disclose the inadequacy of that mode currently held by educators as the dominant view of implementation. I propose an alternative mode of implementation, one that I feel holds promise. Of these two perspectives, one yields a view of implementation as instrumental action; and the other yields a view of implementation as practical action (praxis).

## Implementation as Instrumenal Action

The activity known as 'curriculum implementation' appears to have become a ritual for mainstream educators and is usually conducted in the language of planned rational change. What is the mainstream perspective? I wish to sketch the outlines so that we may gain a fuller view of this perspective, hopefully disclosing at the same time, the embedded view of the teacher.

At a curriculum decision-making conference a few years ago, I was asked to pin-point major issues in the curriculum decision-making process, and I identified as one of the issues 'curriculum implementation'. I argued that, although increasing attention was being given to day-to-day problems of implementation, there has been little attempt to make 'implementation' itself problematic. At that time, I stated the issue as follows (Aoki, 1979:37, 38):

> A basic problem in implementation of programs may be found in the producer-consumer paradigm underlying the view of implementation.

I pointed to this paradigm as one in which curriculum producers give something to curriculum consumers, and added that this paradigm:

> views implementation in terms of a unidirectional flow. It is analogous to the producer-consumer paradigm we have in business and in industry. In this paradigm experts produce for non-experts who consume. It is the paradigm of the relationship between the haves and the have-nots. In program development under this paradigm, curriculum experts produce programs for the consumers – the teachers and students.

> Implementing a program under this paradigm presents a basic problem of how to communicate effectively with people who have not been involved in setting goals, nor in designing resources, nor teaching/learning strategies, nor evaluation plans.

In his recent article, 'Technology versus Craft: A Ten Year Perspective on Innovation', Ernest House (1979) referred to the metaphor 'technological' as being committed to a systematic rationalized approach to change. According to him, the technological perspective flourishes in education underlying not only the notion of implementation, but also the competency-testing movement and the like, spawned as a dimension of the back-to-the-basics curriculum thrust.

Within this view, competence in implementing means to have skills and techniques oriented towards interest in efficient control. Such a know-how-to-do view of competence in implementation is embedded in a scientific and technological thought/action framework, which reduces human competence to instrumental reason and instrumental action. As such, the teacher is seen as a rule-oriented, rule-governed being cast within a manipulative ethos, an ethos in which even the future is conceived in terms of rules.

It is to this kind of phenomenon, dominant in western culture, that men such as Edmund Husserl, Jurgen Habermas, Trent Schroyer, Michael Apple and others have referred as the crisis of western reason. Trent Schroyer (1973) in *The Critique of Domination* speaks of this crisis as reflected in two symbolic events of the sixties, man's landing on the moon and the founding of the Woodstock nation. According to Schroyer, the first, the moon-landing feat, represents the zenith of technical progress; the latter, popular or not, the affirmation of a communal sentiment. These, according to Schroyer, mark a fundamental contradiction between an orientation committed to technological progress and that committed to the improvement of personal and communal life.

Of the two, the paramount mainstream reality seems to be the technological, devoted to the belief that problems and conflicts can be managed through purposive rational action based on precise quantification and systematic decision-making. What is damaging in this approach is the fact that the emphasis on technical strategy as a means of efficient decision-making effectively submerges the ideology of socio-cultural values, and leaves in its wake the 'neutral' standards of purposive rational action, or what could be called 'competence as instrumental reason'.

This same crisis manifests itself as an internal crisis in the field of curriculum as understood by an increasing number of curriculum scholars. Central to this crisis, writ large or small, is the issue of the adequacy of the social theory undergirding it. By social theory I mean the philosophical presuppositions and root metaphors which inform the notion of 'curriculum implementation'. In this sense, I refer to social theoretical idioms of behaviourism, structural functionalism, systems theory, Marxism, neo-Marxism, phenomenology, critical social theory, etc.

To date in the field of education the dominant social theory has been guided by an instrumental notion of reason which impoverishes us by submerging or denying the meaning of cultural reality. By adopting technocratic strategies and allied decision-making social theories, we are asked to admit the rational necessity of extending centralized management theories to more and more areas of the life of teachers, students and administrators in the classroom and the school. This includes implementation. The assumption has been reinforced by positivistic thought, by our 'intoxication' with the technical power of science and technology, and by the development of business management techniques. To question this position requires a radical reexamination of the foundations of social theory and an explanation of alternative modes of inquiry and socio-cultural organization.

That the technological paradigm entrenched among mainstream thought in North America is reflected in the dominance of the R and

D model, more fully elaborated by Egon Guba as the RDDA model – Research, Development, Diffusion and Adoption. Ernest House (1979), considering the RDDA approach within his examination of implementation, has made a telling comment:

> In practice the RDD approach has not worked very well. The federal laboratories and centres have created thousands of new educational products, but these have not been widely used by teachers in the schools. The approach requires the belief that one can create generalizable and easily diffused products that can be used in a great number of settings, a doctrine of transferability.

Despite critiques such as this, two hundred American educators, assembled in Arlington, Virginia, by the National Institute of Education and the US Office of Education, hammered out a 'Statement of Agreement by Professionals in the Field of Educational Dissemination'. This statement which appeared as an editorial in AERA's *Education Researcher* (1977:3) documents 'the consensual beliefs of current professionals in dissemination in education and as such warrants the informed consideration of the R and D community'. In this statement these educators acknowledged multiple meanings of 'dissemination' including 'implementation' defined as 'the facilitation of adoption, adaptation and installation of improvement'. What comes through in reading the document is the non-problematic nature of the R and D paradigm itself; in other words, the R and D paradigm itself was considered as given, not subjected to serious questioning.

In this connection, what ought to be of critical interest to us is Egon Guba's own rejection, after ten years, of his own creation – the RDDA model – for its inadequacies in the field of education. He has raised serious issue with the unified-systems view which, according to him, 'presupposes to effect a linked set of productive agents, each of which assumes discrete responsibility for a segment of R-D-D-A effort to achieve a commonly agreed upon goal' (Guba and Clark, 1977). He argues that this view has set into motion a cycle of failure in educational knowledge production and utilization (KPU) productivity (implementation in other words) by:

1 Establishing unachievable aspirations,
2 Ignoring the idiosyncratic goals of individuals and individual agencies in the KPU community,

3 Changing program directions persistently and frequently in an attempt to overcome failure in achievement provoked by conditions 1 and 2,

4 Over-centralizing and over-controlling programmes which have been assessed as failures.

He calls for a setting aside of the 'unified-system view' and for the reformulation of the conceptual structure based on an authentic sense of 'community'. (Recall my comment about Trent Schroyer's intepretation of Sputnik and Woodstock.) Such a change in metaphor, according to Guba, calls for a change in the language used from systems language to language borrowed from community analysis, for example, instead of 'allocation' and 'authority', 'political' and 'negotiations'; instead of 'delegation' or 'assignment' (congruent with the systems metaphor), 'persuasion'; instead of 'responsibility', 'commitment'. Referring to this communal view, he states (Guba and Clark, 1977:8):

> The configurational view is roughly analogous to the concept of a community. The variety of institutions and individuals concerned with and functioning in educational KPU are more likely to consider themselves to be related to one another in a community sense than an organizational one.

Regarding the rational-logical underpinnings of the unified system view as not being upheld by empirical and experimental examination, he states bluntly: 'The unassailable rational base is not the way the world is'.

We might recall here what Kirkegaard once said: that which is known must be known in a mode appropriate to the thing known. According to this view, implementation as instrumental action is not the way the world is. But in agreeing with them, I feel that more needs to be said about the inadequacy of the instrumental view of implementation.

What is disconcerting is the diverting of the teacher away from the activities of formulating ends, which effectively limits the activities of devising efficient means. What is objectionable is the fact that viewing teachers instrumentally effectively strips them of the humanness of their being, reducing them to beings-as-things, technical beings devoid of their own subjectivity. Reduction to activities within the instrumentalist process renders irrelevant the subjectivity of the teacher. I find such reductive rendering oppressive.

Michael Fullan (1977), a leading scholar in studies of implementation, has referred to the technical ends-means orientation of implementation, where congruence is typically sought between the actually achieved and the intended, as the fidelity model of implementation. Examining major curriculum project activities in Canada and the USA, he pointed to the popularity of this model. One of the projects he referred to is that by Downey and Associates (1975), *Evaluation Study of Elementary and Secondary Schools in Alberta.* He has referred to this study as emphasizing fidelity, for much of the evaluation activities were guided by the central evaluation question posed by the grantors, the Curriculum Branch of the Department. The extent to which the Master Plan for Social Studies was implemented in the schools of Alberta was inevitably construed to be of central relevance to those responsible for the production of the master curriculum. It paid little heed to the relevance structure of the teacher at the other end of the production line. The evaluation team, however, was interested not only in fidelity, but also in the ways in which, in implementation, the teachers were restructuring the master curriculum. But already I am dealing with a non-technical view of the teachers – one that avoids reduction of teacher implementers from beings-as-human to beings-as-things.

In summary then, implementation as instrumental action with the researcher in the locus, involves the following:

Doing curriculum implementation is installing curriculum X.

The interest of the teacher is in placing curriculum X in a classroom or school faithfully and efficiently.

The implied view of curriculum is that of a commodity to be dispensed by teachers and consumed by students.

The implied view of the good teacher is one who installs curriculum X efficiently and faithfully.

To explain 'implementation' within this framework is to give cause-effect relationship.

The implementer's subjectivity is irrelevant as implementing curriculum X is seen as an objective process.

The implied relationship between theory and practice underlying this view of implementation is one in which to implement is to put into practice curriculum-as-plan. (that is, to apply to a practical situation an ideal construct.)

The typical approach to implementation studies is through examination of the degree of fidelity of the installed curriculum compared with the master curriculum.


## Implementation as Practical Action (Praxis)

I would like to try to juxtapose alongside the foregoing view of implementation as instrumental action, a portrayal of another view of competence in implementing, an alternative which I claim portrays 'implementation as practical action' or 'implementation as praxis'.

In using the term 'practice' as 'praxis', I am reminded of Paulo Freire's (1972:205–206) remarks:

> All education practice implies a theoretical stance on the educator's part. This stance in turn implies – sometimes more, sometimes less explicitly – an interpretation of man and the world. It could not be otherwise.

I am mindful that Freire is not referring to a dualistic notion of 'practice and theory', wherein 'practice' is viewed as 'applied theory', nor wherein practice is viewed a-theoretically separated from theory. I feel that the separation of theory and practice, allowing us to view practice as 'applied theory' or as a-theoretical practice, has prevented us from theorizing about practice.

In my endeavour to reconceive implementation, allow me to shift my attention to the notion of 'competence in implementing'. To move towards the uncovering of an alternative view, let us explore the root etymology of the term 'competence'. Disclosure of the Latin root openly reveals not only the original view but a fresh view as well. The Latin root is 'com-petere': 'com' meaning 'together', and 'petere' meaning 'to seek'. In a root sense, then, 'to be competent' means 'to be able to seek together' or 'to be able to venture forth together'. This root meaning of 'competence' as 'communal venturing' holds promise for reviewing what it means to be a teacher competent in implementing curriculum (Aoki, 1980).

I now seek support from a phenomenological scholar whose work I have only recently come to know. He is a Polish scholar, by the name of Karol Wojtyla, who speaks, of course, in a context broader than that of education. (We know him as Pope John Paul II). His denouncement of competence as instrumental action has meaningful relevance to our search. I understand that Wojtyla became skeptical of the reductive tendencies of instrumental reason embedded in materialistic and positivistic thought, inherited from the nineteenth century which spread pervasively into most domains of thought in Poland. He recognized that since Descartes, knowledge of man and his world has been identified with cognition, and the ensuing post-Cartesian attitude extended it as is reflected in behaviourism, utilitarianism and determinism. His efforts to transcend objectivism appear in his book *The Acting Person* (Wojtyla, 1979) which deals with the communal venturing of persons as they experience life through action and reflection upon their own experiences. Unravelling the network of man's constitutive tendencies and strivings, Wojtyla, in his book, attempted to reveal man's status in the world, the meaning of emancipation and of human fulfillment. He probed, by means of ontological hermeneutics, the constitutive dynamism integrated by the acting person. Believing that man is no mere creature of circumstances, conditioned and encapsulated by his social milieu, he proposed man's worthy life venture as self-disclosure and self-governance as he fashions a personal and social life worth living. By emphasizing both the communal condition of man and the irreducible transcendence of the human person with respect to the current of social life, he counteracted the reductionist tendencies so prevalent in contemporary philosophy and culture. Furthermore, he saw man as a historical being, man as a maker of his own history, who together with others are seen as co-makers of history.

I wish to interpret Wojtyla's remarks within the micro-community of the classroom, wherein dwell students, teacher and curriculum X to be implemented. Within such a communal situation, competence in implementing curriculum X may be seen as a dialectical relationship among teachers, students and curriculum X, mediated by everyday language and oriented towards practical interest in establishing open and non-violent subjectivity on which authentic communication depends. These dialectic interactions are rooted in the network of interpretive meanings given by the actors within that situation. Included will be the meanings that the teacher and students give to curriculum X. Hence, understanding the day-to-day life of teachers and students in the classroom where curriculum X is being implemented requires at least understanding in terms of the meaning actors in the classroom give to curriculum X.

This action based in mutual understanding of meaning structures is what Michael Fullan means by implementation as mutual adaptation. However, to be able to venture forth together with curriculum X in the meaningful way Wojtyla speaks of requires not only a mutual understanding of this meaning structure but also action upon curriculum X rooted in critical reflection of these meaning structures.

I would like to interpret what I can now refer to as critical venturing together more concretely within a classroom framework. The teacher with curriculum X interprets curriculum X as he or she allows students to enter his or her interpretive framework while he or she engages him/herself with students mutually in interpretive activities. But for these activities to be critical, there must be a reflective turn. There needs to be a break in the direct experiences, a distancing as it were, to reflect upon what it is that makes it possible for them to think and act as they are thinking and acting.

For a group of teachers involved in implementing curriculum X, what may be more meaningful is for them to enter into dialogical situations with their colleagues also engaged in interpreting curriculum X. The enriched community of teachers with their multiple interpretations provide opportunities for a reciprocity of teacher interpretations. Such an activity provides opportunities for mutual reflection. But what must be remembered is that joint reflection upon these many interpretations may result in mere coming to know of one another's interpretive meanings, that is, the teachers may reach an understanding of curriculum implementation merely as multiple realities, content within the moral posture of 'pluralism'. What is needed is for these curriculum implementers to take a critical posture to help one another disclose, by bringing into fuller view the deep structure of meanings, that is, their own assumptions and intentions, as they interpret the curriculum and act with it and upon it.

In this critical moment, it is important for our teacher implementers to remember that a critical perspective is a two-bladed knife, cutting both ways. As Werner (1978) states:

> We must be reflective of the very perspective we use for critical sense-making. Any clarifying of perspective of others ... is itself perspective guided. In arguing for point-of-viewism one cannot presume himself free of a viewpoint. One way to deal with this dilemma is to make explicit and reflect upon the theoretical, and methodological beliefs within which our own thinking and acting are situated.

Thus, in critical reflection, each of our teachers needs to place his/her everyday type of attitude in 'brackets' as it were, and examine it in an attempt to go beyond the immediate level of interpretation. In this sense, critical reflection and action is thoughtful action; that is, action full of thought, and thought full of action. Critical reflection thus leads to an understanding of what is beyond. Such reflectivity allows disclosure of tacitly held assumptions and intentions of the authors of curriculum X, which likely have not been explicitly given. Or such reflectivity allows disclosure of the teacher's own unconsciously held assumptions and intentions that underlie his or her interpretation of curriculum X. Either or both of these may be repressive constraints which the teacher needs to face. For example, the content of reflection may be the 'rationalization' the teacher uses to hide underlying motives for his own action, or it may be the 'ideology' used by those who developed curriculum X, rendering obscure the developer's interests that lie beneath. In this sense critical reflection demonstrates interest in discovering the hidden 'true interests' embedded in some given humanly lived situation.

Reflection, however, is not only oriented towards making conscious the unconscious by disclosing underlying assumptions and intentions, but it is also oriented towards the implications for action guided by the newly gained critical knowing. It is interested in bringing about a reorientation through clarification of the assumptions and intentions upon which thought and action rest. These may be preconceived norms, values, images of man and world, assumptions about knowledge, root metaphors and perspectives. Competence in implementation of curriculum X as critical venturing together has an interest in liberating the teacher from hidden assumptions and intentions of both themselves and curriculum X, promoting a social theory grounded in the moral attitude of liberation and improvement.

To summarize, where implementation occurs as practical action with the teacher as the locus the following occur:

> Within this framework, doing curriculum implementation is to come to a deep understanding of curriculum X and transforming it based on the appropriateness to the situation.

> The implementer's interest is in the transformation of curriculum X within the situation based on disclosed underlying assumptions and conditions that make the transformation possible.

> The implied view of curriculum X is that it is an object to be interpreted, and critically reflected upon in an on-going transformation of curriculum and self.

> The implied view of the teacher is that of an actor who acts with and upon curriculum X as he/she reflects upon his/her own assumptions underlying action.

Within this framework to explain implementation is to trace to underlying unreflected aspects which upon disclosure imply transformative action.

The interpreter's central activity is reflection upon his subjectively based action with and upon curriculum X.

The implied form of theory/practice relationship is that theory and practice are in dialectic relationship. To implement within this framework is to reflect critically upon the relationship between curriculum-as-plan and curriculum-in-use.

To evaluate implementation within this framework is to examine the quality of the activity of discovering underlying assumptions, interests, values, motives, perspectives, root metaphors and implications for action to improve the human condition.

## Conclusions

What I have attempted in this chapter is to portray implementation using the categorical distinction between 'technique' and 'praxis'; that is, between instrumental action and practical action, between beings-as-things and beings-as-humans, signifying two frames of reference in which the reality of implementation activity can be constituted.

In the framework of 'technique' (instrumental action), implementation is objectified; that is, it is constituted as action according to nomological laws. Competence in implementation within this framework assumes actions of beings-as-things oriented toward interest in control, efficiency and certainty. In contrast, in the framework of 'praxis' (practical action), implementation is constituted by the inter-subjective actions of beings-as-humans, oriented towards cognitive interest in mutual understanding and, also, the practical interest in securing authentically the always precarious intersubjectivity. In this framework competence in implementation is seen as competence in communicative action and reflection, and the reality of curriculum X is constituted or reconstituted within a community of actors and speakers.

Within the framework of 'praxis' and emancipating actions, these actors and speakers are oriented towards 'de-naturalizing' that which commonsense declares to be human nature; they explore and condemn the commonsensical dismissal of alternate realities, and they attempt to restore the legitimacy of those existential issues which commonsense, following human historical predicament, pulverizes into a multitude of mini-problems as can be articulated in purely instrumental terms.

Ultimately, competence in implementation as praxis, as I have outlined it, is for people who find unacceptable the way competence in implementation is known by mainstream America. In essence, critical competence in implementation is the metaphor we choose to oppose inhumanity. Hence, if a school is a community of human beings, there is no question on my part that there is no place in school for implementation viewed as instrumental action. What we need is action that humanizes. Implementation as praxis is one such mode of action.

## References

AERA (1977) 'Editorial: Statement of agreement by professionals in the field of educational dissemination' *Educational Researcher* November.

AOKI, T. (1974) 'Pin-pointing issues in curriculum decision-making' *Curriculum Decision Making in Alberta: A Janus Look* Alberta Department of Education, Alberta, Canada.

AOKI, T. (1979) *Toward a Curriculum Inquiry in a New Key* Occasional Paper No 2, Edmonton Department of Secondary Education, University of Alberta.

AOKI, T. (1980) Competence as Instrumental Action and as Practical Action. An invited paper presented at *The Curriculum Conference on Competence* held in May 18–20, 1980 at Pernnsylvania State University, University City, Pennsylvania.

DOWNEY, L. and ASSOCIATES (1975) *Evaluation Study of Elementary and Secondary Schools in Alberta* Alberta Department of Education, Alberta, Canada.

FREIRE, P. (1972) *The Pedagogy of the Oppressed* New York, Herder and Herder.

FULLAN, M. and POMFRET, A. (1977) 'Research on curriculum and instruction implementation' *Review of Educational Research* Winter 47(1).

GUBA, E. and CLARK, C. (1977) 'The configurational perspective: A new view of educational knowledge production and utilization' *Educational Researcher* April.

HOUSE, E. (1979) 'Technology versus craft: A ten year perspective on innovation' *Journal of Curriculum Studies* 11(1).

SCHROYER, T. (1973) *The Critique of Domination: The Origins and Development of Critical Theory* Boston, Beacon Press.

WERNER, W. (1978) 'Evaluation: Sense-making of school program' in AOKI, T. (Ed) *Curriculum Evaluation in a New Key* University of British Columbia, Centre for the Study of Curriculum and Instruction.

WOJTYLA, K. (1979) *The Acting Person* Boston, D. Reidel Publishing Co.

# Assisting Schools to Develop School-Focused Action Programmes

Ken Eltis, John Braithwaite, Christine Deer,
Harry Kensell
Macquarie University, Australia

## Introduction

'How do schools rejuvenate themselves?' is a question that has challenged writers, researchers and educational administrators for many years. Usually the renewal of schools as effective learning institutions has been attempted through the provision of traditional inservice courses run on a short-term basis, wherein individual teachers are introduced to new ideas and/or methods. Such an approach fails to consider the complexity of schools as organizations, and the educational return to the *total* school of individual teachers attending such courses, has been marginal to say the least. A number of alternative approaches to fostering total or school-based rejuvenation has been tried, including the establishment of a mutual support network for principals (*cf* Bentzen, 1974), selective withdrawal of school personnel for longer term courses (*cf* Sieber, 1981) and fostering informal approaches incorporating the use of teachers' centres (*cf* Kahn, 1972). However, such approaches usually have only a short-term effect and their total impact upon schools is usually minimal.

The reasons for the comparative failure of these approaches in helping schools to help themselves, have been documented by a number of writers. Generally, they refer to the complexity of schools as organizations retarding effective whole school responses to issues; the lack of time and resources for such programmes; negative attitudes on the part of the schools' hierarchies and teacher apathy (*cf* Bailey and Braithwaite, 1980; Baker and Sikora, 1981; Davies, 1981). Official reports into teacher education have long recognized the advantages to be derived from schools identifying their own needs and developing programmes to meet such needs, while at the same time they have highlighted the problems confronting the effective implementation of such programs (*cf* James, 1972; Taylor, 1978; Batten, 1979; Auchmuty, 1980; Correy, 1980).

The difficulty with the concept of school-focused in-service education is that educational policy makers have not provided sufficient resources to permit schools to develop programmes in ways that would overcome many of the known difficulties with school-focused in-service education. At a time when educational authorities in most Western countries are finding that resources are becoming more limited, it does appear necessary to investigate alternative approaches to fostering school-focused in-service education, for as the 1975 Report of the Australian Schools Commission noted, 'perhaps the most important single grouping for development activities is the total group within the school' (Schools Commission, 1975, 185). The concept is clearly worth fostering if schools are to be helped to become more effective educational agencies. The major problem in this area appears to be that, given limited resources, how do we help schools to help themselves?

As one way of investigating the issue, a group of teacher educators at an Australian university set out to determine whether their skills and knowledge could assist three metropolitan secondary schools in Sydney to identify own needs and develop programmes to meet these needs. Essentially, the study was an attempt to use existing resources to guide schools in the development of school-focused inservice programmes.

## The Present Project

In October 1980, a one-year study was initiated to provide information about what happened when three secondary schools established the beginnings of an effective school development programme while collaborating with staff from a tertiary institution. The Project had three objectives:

1   to assist secondary schools in the development, implementation and evaluation of school-focused inservice education policies;

2   to monitor the processes followed by the school staffs and the supporting tertiary institution in developing these policies:

3   to prepare guidelines about the development of school-focused in-service programmes for use by similar educational institutions.

Two government coeducational secondary schools in one Metropolitan Region of New South Wales and one all boys' secondary school nominated by the Sydney Catholic Education Office were involved. How these schools analyzed their needs and arrived at suggestions for a development programme was the initial focus of the Project. Of particular importance was the active role four members of the staff from the School of Education in a University might play. Collectively, they set out to play a consultative and collaborative role with each of the schools and to help the schools to analyze their needs and structure programmes to meet them.

Funding for the Project ($15,000) was provided by the Australian Schools Commission. From the total sum, each school had a grant of $1250 to use in facilitating school-focused in-service as part of the Project. Schools were to use this money as they saw appropriate. The bulk of the total grant was used to cover the salary of a research assistant employed on a three-day per week basis.

## Stages in the Development of the Project

There were three clear stages in the Project, the *negotiation*, the *initiation* and the *action* phases. Item 1 summarizes the activities in each stage.

In *the negotiation phase*, which lasted from October, 1979 to October, 1980, lengthy preliminary discussions were held with officers from the Schools Commission. When it became apparent that the Project was seen by the Commission as having the potential to provide valuable information about school-focused in-service, discussions began in May, 1980, with the NSW Department of Education and the Sydney Catholic Education Office.

By the time funding was made available in October, 1980, not only had discussions been held with members of the State Development Committee, Sydney Catholic Education Office and the relevant Regional Director of Education, but also the schools which might be approached had been suggested by the relevant Authorities.

The necessity to embark upon such lengthy negotiation is often overlooked by those wanting to work in schools and by many writers on the theme of desirable practices in relation to school-focused development programmes. But the goodwill that developed between the Project team and the various educational personnel during the negotiation phase proved highly valuable over the ensuing months.

*The initiation stage*, continuing over three months, was the time when contacts were made with the staffs in the three schools which

*Item 1    Overview of the Project's Activities*

| Date | | Activities |
|---|---|---|
| October 1979 | N | Discussions with – |
| | E | |
| | G | .Schools Commission |
| | O | .Officers from NSW Department of Education |
| | T | .Sydney Catholic Education Office |
| | I | .Members of State Development Committee |
| | A | .Regional Director |
| | T | |
| | I | |
| | O | |
| | N | |
| October 1980 | | Funding approved |
| | | Permission given to approach schools |
| | | Research Assistant appointed |
| October 1980 | I | Approaches to Schools |
| | N | |
| | I | .Agreement |
| | T | .Needs Survey and Analysis |
| | I | .Interviews with Staff |
| | A | .Report to Schools |
| | T | |
| | I | |
| | O | |
| | N | |
| December 1980 | | |
| February 1981 | | Committees Established |
| | | Schools decide on Priorities |
| March 1981 | A | *PROGRAMS* |
| | C | |
| | T | School A    School B    School C |
| | I | |
| | O | |
| | N | |
| September 1981 | | |

had been nominated for the Project. Having had preliminary discussions with the School Principal in each case, it was agreed that a member of the Project team should outline the objectives of the Project to the staffs of each school and invite participation. This was a particularly difficult time for the Project for it required the team to take a non-directive approach as they set about describing 'it' (that is, the development programme) to staff members. The 'it' was not yet discernible to teachers, for the 'it' depended upon a subsequent 'needs analysis' that the school staffs were to carry out with the aid of the Project team if agreement to participate in the Project was forth-coming.

All three schools agreed to participate in the 'needs analysis'. There were two phases to the action at this point. A brief questionnaire was given to staff in each school asking them to identify needs on a whole school, departmental, and a personal basis. When the results of this survey had been analyzed, interviews were set up with about one-third of the staff in each of the government schools and two-thirds in the non-government school. These interviews, each of about thirty minutes, were designed to clarify issues raised in the survey and enable the Project team to develop a clear understanding of the school and its needs as defined by staff. Staff chosen for interview represented a cross-section of each school. As a result of the interviews a ranking was obtained of the expressed needs.

These two approaches, then, formed part of the preliminary step in designing school-focused development programmes based on an analysis of needs. The reporting of these analyses convinced each school of the merit in developing in-service programmes to meet its own specialized needs.

The final stage of the Project, *the action phase*, lasted over nine months and saw the development of specific in-service programmes within each school. To facilitate liaison with Project members and to coordinate activities within each school, staff committees were established. The membership of these committees, in terms of representing a balance between school executives and teachers, varied from school to school. Subsequent experiences confirmed the vital roles these committees were to play in the effectiveness of the Project's *action* phase.

Proposals for action programmes within each school, based on the needs analyses, are shown in Item 2. In general, it can be readily seen that the topics suggested by the school staffs covered the most immediate needs of large secondary schools. Because of the relatively short funding period, only the first listed need in each case was isolated for consideration in the initial stages of the action phase.

Each school's committee decided to organize programmes on a 'whole school' basis rather than on traditional subject/faculty lines. This seemed a logical move as the basic assumption underlying the Project was that it should result in the examination of problems whose resolution would lead to overall school improvement. In planning subsequent programmes, the resources of the University and the individual expertise and contacts of the Project team were made available to each school.

All committees decided to stage a series of workshops to initiate discussion and to examine alternatives for action. These were held at

*Item 2:    Perceived Needs on Whole School Basis For Each of the Three Schools*\*

---

*School A*
Government Coeducational Secondary School
1.  Democracy in Schools
2.  Teaching Unstreamed Classes
3.  Evaluation and Assessment
4.  Transition Education
5.  Teacher, Student and the Law
6.  School Philosophy
7.  Subject Integration

*School B*
Government Coeducational Secondary School
1.  Communication
2.  Discipline
3.  Evaluation
4.  Special Needs Programmes
5.  Transition Education
6.  Problems of Pupil Isolation
7.  Improved Academic Performance
8.  Encouraging Parent Involvement

*School C*
Non-Government Boys' Secondary School
1.  Language Skills
2.  Discipline
3.  Evaluation and Assessment
4.  Alternative Curriculum/Transition Education
5.  Teaching Religion

---

\* Needs are given in priority order

varying times. Within the two government schools meetings were held at recess, lunch or after school. The non-government school was more fortunate in that its meetings could be held in designated in-service time when pupils were dismissed from their classes.

It has to be emphasized that the Project had a very limited life-span of one year. It ended just as extensive activity was evident in at least two of the three schools. In one school, for example, the Project led to data-gathering from staff, students and parents on school aims and the results then led to consideration of a reformulation of policy emphases for the school. (When funding for the Project ceased, contact between the school and the University continued and moves are still under way to have the school, parents, students and the University team members all participate in workshops to produce new aims and policies for the school.) In another school, by the end of the Project the focus had been shifted to school curriculum development for Years 7 and 8 and it is planned that this, in turn, will flow on to the preparation of revised programmes for the rest of the school. In these cases, at least, experience in whole school development programmes has led to the tackling of further problems. In this way the Project provided a vital (if not necessary) stimulus to subsequent curriculum development.

Essentially the Project was an action programme and no attempt was made to design a research study with relatively few, tightly controlled variables. Each school made its own response to the demands of the Project and then fostered its development throughout the year. Both Project members and school committees were responsible for the evaluation of the various activities. Information for the evaluation came from three areas: observation, interviews and questionnaires. As well, documentary information was gathered in relation to each activity and from the various workshops and committee meetings. The data gathered were incorporated in a detailed case study describing and assessing what happened in each school.

## Outcomes of the Project

It will be recalled that a principal objective of the Project was to prepare guidelines relating to the development of school-focused in-service programmes to assist schools and tertiary institutions collaborating in such a venture. The discussion which follows concentrates on the implications for schools. Implications for tertiary institutions are discussed in detail elsewhere (see Eltis, Braithwaite, Deer and Kensell, 1981).

## Implications for School Personnel

The project approach adopted was new to school personnel. While the presentation of the Project created some confusion, even misgivings, as staff were not used to being encouraged to express openly their views on what general school problems they perceived to exist and what should be done to attend to them, there can be little doubt that the conducting of the Project in all three schools had considerable impact. The study led to important discussions of key issues in each school. In two schools these discussions resulted in surveys to determine what new priorities might be set for school goals and, in the third, new programmes are being developed for an integrated curriculum covering the first two years of the high school. School organization was also affected as committees were set up which cut across the traditional lines of a subject-based executive responsible for decision-making in the school. In these committees the significant role of the committee coordinator/convenor emerged as an important factor in helping to sustain the action. Where the coordinator was effective the committees operated with positive results. The nature of the skills required by committee members also became apparent in the course of the Project.

Staffs in the three schools were used to decisions being made about matters affecting the school either by the Principal, or the Principal in consultation with the Deputy and subject department heads. As well, teachers were used to being considered as belonging to a particular group of subject teachers wherein the line of communication proceeded downward from the executive to the staff through the subject department heads. What the Project demonstrated, as it developed in each school, is that such lines of communication tend to isolate teachers in their individual subject areas. This isolation is often exacerbated in New South Wales schools as staff study units tend to be organized on a teaching-subject basis. As well, it soon became apparent how difficult it is to get teachers to think across subject boundaries and see matters from a 'total school' perspective. The initial interviews conducted as part of the needs survey revealed how little staff knew of what teachers in other areas were doing. It is not surprising, then, that staff appreciated the workshops in the programme that were organized on a cross-faculty basis, especially when they heard what other teachers in other fields did to cope with problems they also were trying to resolve. These workshops demonstrated that it is possible to shift the focus of attention to matters affecting the whole school and to improve school communication as a result. However, the resistance to this kind of regrouping of staff should not be underestimated. But, without it, school-focused INSET, which concentrates on matters affecting the whole school population, cannot succeed.

*In each school a committee was established* to liaise with the Project team. One of the crucial tasks for each committee was motivating school staffs to focus on whole school issues, breaking down the barriers caused by the subject department organization of secondary schools.

The rate of progress in each school was closely related to the effectiveness of the committee. This is not to conclude, however, that the basic cause of slow progress was necessarily the committee. Rather, the operational effectiveness of each committee might be seen as a reflection of many favourable or unfavourable factors in the respective schools.

The committees succeeded best in those schools where they had the power to act and where there was an absence of well-established, non-formal cliques which could detract from the Project's progress. This was a crucial factor. In the school where the constant expectation was that no support would be given by the Principal or the executive, least was achieved during the year. Power can come in two ways. Either the Principal can lay down firm guidelines concerning the areas where the committee might make decisions and the committee operates within these parameters, or she/he can decide to be represented on the committee to ensure that the Principal's views are known and taken into account as decisions are made. While the Principal in New South Wales secondary schools has the right to review proposed actions, actions are more likely to occur if his/her views are known to the committee. On this point, however, the vital position of the Principal must be noted. To some extent the Principal is vulnerable and open to criticism if she/he chooses to overturn a decision taken by a committee. It is important then that good relations be maintained between the Principal and the committee to promote a positive school climate.

Crucial to the committee's efficient operation is its membership. As school-focused INSET involves consideration of whole school issues, the committee should be representative of the whole school staff. Membership should cut across traditional subject-based groupings, contain experienced and less experienced staff and have some of the school's executive amongst its members to provide additional input and guidance. While it is true to say that initial progress in this Project was most rapid in the school where the committee consisted of a large number of authority figures, in the long run the school in which the committee had a blending of powerful figures and younger staff saw the most striking developments. The school in which the committee had no obvious support from the powerful members of the school executive and where younger teachers predominated, made the least progress.

Committee members need to be aware at the outset that their work will be difficult and time-consuming. The very nature of their task – to determine how to conduct a needs analysis and devise suitable programmes in response to their review – presents problems. Staff, who are busy people, may well object to 'extra' demands being made on their time and if these demands come from what they perceive to be a light-weight, unimportant committee they will not be taken seriously. But of no less importance is the threat the committees might pose to the traditional power base in secondary schools, the executive. Without their support little will be achieved. Hence the importance of having members of the executive actively involved in the work of the committee, not just for their experience and likely greater expertise in decision-making but also because they provide an essential link with the group which usually has an important say in final decisions.

So far the discussion has centred on who should be on the committee and why. The skills required by committee members should also be considered. It was the Project team's view that in all schools committee members generally displayed little experience when it came to organizing and conducting meetings. A key problem was that often no-one appeared to be in charge, so the tasks before committee members were not clearly defined before being allocated to members for action. The teachers were simply not used to accepting responsibility for arriving at group decisions which would lead to action. Even the recording of minutes at a meeting posed a problem. In the one school where set times were laid down for meetings (a time being set aside on the school timetable) and a coordinator was given an assigned role, swift progress was made. Where committees operated on an *ad hoc* and somewhat more casual basis, progress was much slower.

Reviewing the Project, it is now clear that a very careful analysis must be made at the outset to determine the existence and level of relevant skills amongst committee members. Skills important to the successful implementation of a Project of this kind include knowing how to set priorities, the management of meetings, committee decision-making and accurate and appropriate communication at all levels. All of this reflection suggests that once a committee has been formed there is a need for members to be given an introductory programme not just to familiarize them with the aims of the Project but also with the kinds of demands to be made of them. High on the agenda for such an introductory programme must be how to conduct meetings and then cope with the task of liaising with staff at all levels. For such a programme to be effective committee members should be freed from teaching commitments at given times, a small price to pay in the interests of ensuring successful programme development.

Finally, how should committee members be chosen? It could be concluded that the formation of committees in the participating schools was, in general, a fairly haphazard exercise which may have been more productive had it been more carefully controlled. On the other hand, the apparent haphazard development of the committees provided some valuable insights into basic conflicts in the schools. Ultimately the Principal will have to oversee the formation of the committee (thought not necessarily be a member). Here the Principal has the chance to encourage younger members of staff, not forming part of the school executive but wanting to make a valuable contribution, to play a significant role. The experience younger staff gain in such a capacity will be invaluable, especially as they see how difficult it is to win approval and support from a large secondary school staff with so many competing demands and interests. The most vital decision which the Principal has to make is who should be the coordinator of the activity and chair the committee.

*The key person in the development of school-focused INSET is the school coordinator or committee convener.* In the two schools where most progress was made there was a person clearly designated to carry out the task and the work of the committee benefited because of his influence. In one of these schools the coordinator was a power figure in the school, the Deputy Principal; in the other school, the project coordinator was not a member of the executive but had taught for eight years and was considered to be on top of his teaching subject. While he expressed reservations about going outside his own field of subject expertise and about his ability to handle the task, he 'grew in the job' and responded well to the responsibility placed on him.

The coordinator's task is not an easy one. At a basic level she/he needs to be able to organize and conduct meetings, helping the committee to arrive at decisions which must then be followed up. She/he must then be able to communicate with staff at large to ensure that they know what the committee is doing. Thus this person must project an image which indicates that she/he is not just a teacher of a subject but can cope with broader responsibilities affecting the life of the school. This person must also win the confidence of the executive who can undermine her/his work and that of the committee if they do not value her/his efforts.

Finally, she/he has a further liaison role with those who will assist in the INSET programme. Such people may come from within the school, in which case the coordinator must know the talents of the staff; or they may be sought from outside the school. In the present Project it was this link with the school coordinator which proved so valuable to the Project team at all stages and to the ultimate success of the Project in each school. Once the coordinators had faith in the abilities of the Project team, negotiations became much easier and the pace of development quickened. As well, coordinators could advise the external consultants on how action might best proceed, where obstacles might be encountered and what additional help would be required. This facilitating function was essential to the Project's success.

It is clear from the present study that there is a need for a clearly designated position occupied by someone likely to win the respect of all staff and having the ability to initiate action which will require their support. This includes the ability to run staff workshops. The coordinator, then, must be mature, confident, articulate and not lacking in interpersonal skills. The coordinator must know the staff well, be respected and be competent as a teacher. As the task makes so many demands on the person, time allowance should be given to ensure that the role is effectively carried out.

*From experience in this Project it is apparent that all schools would benefit from having a coordinator for INSET, able to work across the school and to contribute to the development of school policy on matters transcending subject department boundaries.* Whether this coordinator position should be an established promotion position or not is an open question. There is merit in leaving it to the school (and the Principal) to decide who should fill the post and for how long. It certainly provides younger members of staff with an opportunity to gain valuable experience in coping with programme development affecting the whole school staff. Whether the coordinator position should also involve a responsibility beyond INSET (that is, to include initial training and induction tasks, as suggested in the United Kingdom, Bolan, 1980) is also an open question. Judging from the experiences in each of the three Project Schools, coordinators will have no shortage of tasks when implementing school-focused activities.

## Suggested Guidelines for Developing and Implementing School-Focused In-service Programmes

The following guidelines emerged from the present Project as ways likely to enhance the success of school-focused in-service programmes. No attempt is made here to consider how a tertiary institution might prepare its staff for involvement in school-focused in-service. But an assumption in the guidelines is that there is a willingness on the part of a school staff to work with external consultants in implementing a programme. Nor has consideration been given to where the impetus for a programme of this kind might originate. It may come from a school which has seen the need to look beyond its own walls to outsiders who might provide additional insights and expertise. It may come as the result of an initiative on the part of the tertiary institution wanting to extend its involvement in continuing teacher education. It is also assumed that some form of discussion will have taken place between the school and the tertiary personnel. (Ideally, the tertiary INSET coordinator will have selected appropriate staff and will have made arrangements for suitable tertiary consultants to be released from some of their normal teaching commitments so they can maintain a heavy involvement with the school.)

Whatever the source of the initiative, schools and tertiary personnel should benefit from a consideration of the following procedures which incorporate the experiences gained in the three secondary schools participating in the present Project.

1 *Appointment of a School Coordinator*
   The person who is to take on this role must be able to cope with the broad responsibilities associated with offering leadership to the whole school. The Coordinator should therefore be mature, be known for her/his good interpersonal skills and be respected for her/his capacity as a classroom teacher. Consideration might be given to having this person elected by the staff for a given period (for example two years).

2   *Establishment of a School In-service Committee*
The Principal, in consultation with the Coordinator, should establish a committee which is representative of the school staff. Membership should cut across traditional subject-based groupings in the school and contain a blend of experienced and less-experienced staff. To give it weight in the school, the committee should also contain some of the school executive. When choosing committee members care should be taken to ensure that the members are willing to be involved and are committed. Continual changes in membership undermine the workings of a committee, though it is understandable that, as the range of activities changes so, too, will committee membership.

3   *Establishing Guidelines for the Coordinator and the Committee*
The Principal must make clear to the committee what support they can expect. It is essential for the committee and the Coordinator to know just how much power they have. They must also know what they can expect by way of release time for meetings and planning activities. Members also need to be allocated specific tasks, for example, drawing up agendas, keeping minutes, putting up notices for the staff. If such duties are not specific the committee will not function smoothly, nor will it meet regularly.
The Principal should also ensure that necessary timetable changes are made to allow the committee to meet regularly.

4   *Initial Meeting of Committee and External Consultants*
Such a meeting should take place immediately after the committee has been formed to discuss what school-focused INSET involves and how action might best be initiated. This meeting will be assisted if the school Coordinator, the school Principal and the external consultants have preliminary discussions on what cooperation can be expected throughout the programme.
To ensure that this meeting is successful, the Coordinator and the consultants should carefully plan an agenda and all committee members should be freed from teaching. This will be the first sign to all that the program will receive tangible support in a positive way – the provision of time to plan.
It will be important to consider at this stage what the staff's

likely attitude to school-focused INSET will be and to try
to anticipate their questions.

5 *Presentation to the Staff*

At the initial meeting with the staff adequate time has to be
set aside for explanation of what school-focused INSET is,
what it will involve for the staff, which kinds of programmes might be evolved, and how. Staff must also have
an adequate opportunity for questions. The first meeting is
of vital importance to the staff. It must be carefully timed;
early afternoon dismissal of students would be advan-
tageous so staff can concentrate on the matters for discussion and not have their mind on the next lesson or on the
need to rush off to playground duty. On this occasion a first
attempt might even be made to organize cross-faculty
discussion groups to discuss issues raised in the presentation. If this is attempted, group leaders need to be appointed
and briefed as to what they are to do in their groups and
how they should report to staff. Committee members from
the school could perform this role and the whole meeting
could be run by the Coordinator. This would ensure high
visibility for those staff members in their new role as
committee members.

A contribution from the external consultants should also
form part of the initial presentation so they can be seen by
staff to be playing an important role. They could help with
explanations during the presentation and then assist group
leaders. In this way they can begin to establish their identity
and credibility not just with the committee but also with the
staff at large.

If it turns out that adequate time has not been set aside, a
further review meeting should be held before moving to the
needs analysis.

6 *Conducting the Needs Analysis*

Questionnaires should be prepared by the committee to ask
staff to indicate their needs at a number of levels

whole school
functional group
individual.

When the questionnaires have been analyzed, arrangements
should then be made to interview a sample of the staff. The
Coordinator should select this sample to cover all subject

areas and incorporating older and younger teachers, including those new to the school. The external consultants should play an active part in interviewing.

7 *Feedback of Information to Staff*
The committee should ensure that it informs the staff as quickly as possible of what the needs survey showed. It is possible, on the basis of experience in the present Project, to complete this task within five-six weeks of the initial presentation to the staff. At this stage the committee should indicate when it intends to meet and how it hopes to proceed. Staff should bε encouraged to talk informally to committee members who, by this stage should be well known to everyone. Certainly the Coordinator can now see to it that she/he liaises with staff and hears their views.

8 *Consideration of a Possible Programme in Response to Needs*
By now the committee will have a formidable task. It must decide what the school can cope with and devise a programme which balances programmes designed to meet 'whole school' needs against programmes designed to meet 'functional group' needs. As well, attention will need to be directed at how to balance single intensive activities against ongoing, developmental activities which will continue for some time in the school.
The committee must make a realistic appraisal of the time available each week both for the committee to coordinate activities and for the staff to be involved in school-focused programmes. A further key factor for the committee to consider will be when to hold programmes. If possible, workshops should be arranged in such a way that, at the beginning, they make few additional demands on teacher time outside school hours. The scheduling of programmes able to be attended by all staff presents a major difficulty for the committee. At this stage full use should be made of funds to obtain relief teachers and release staff from their normal duties.
The committee must also make a sound appraisal of the talents on the school staff. It will be helpful to use staff who can made a valuable contribution to any workshop activity that is set up. In this way schools can see that the resolution of problems is often best found amongst it own staff.

As well, tertiary consultants should also be able to make suggestions concerning who might help in the presentation of programmes. They should undertake to introduce possible providers to the school committee or the Coordinator so that, as providers, they are fully aware of what will be expected of them.

9  *Implementation of Programmes*
Once a decision has been made as to the kind of programme best fitted to a significant school need and most likely to have a major impact on the staff, action should follow. Again, committee members should play an active role. The kind of cross-faculty groups suggested above (see point 5) may assist in helping the staff to see things from a perspective which is not bound to their own teaching subject.

10  *Sustaining the Action*
Throughout, the Coordinator and the Committee should see to it that the Principal and staff are kept fully informed of progress being made and of appropriate lines of development. Full use should be made of staff morning teas, staff meetings and bulletin boards. The introduction of a newsletter may also help communication.

11  *Evaluating the Effort*
Throughout, the committee needs to determine what steps should be taken to have the action programme evaluated. Evaluation should consist of a review of the programme offered, the processes followed in presenting it, and the impact of the offering. Committee members need to remain alert to the need to listen to staff and receive their comments.
At a more formal level, use may be made of the tertiary consultants to attempt more detailed evaluation.
It will be essential for the committee to consider the results of evaluation and report them to both the Principal and the staff. It will also be important for the committee to review its own efforts and decide where it has been inefficient and where other practices might be introduced.

Our project demonstrated that much can be achieved within a limited budget. If the guidelines suggested above are followed using within-school development grants (in New South Wales now increased to an amount up to $2000 Australian) a very worthwhile programme can be mounted. Each of the participating schools received $1250 (Australian) and no school exhausted its funds in the twelve months. The major item of expenditure was money to provide teacher release time enabling committee members to be freed to attend planning meetings and organize workshops. It is essential that schools continue to have access to such funding so teachers can be freed from their teaching commitments at regular intervals to meet and plan activities for the school. Throughout the year the complaint was constant that teachers did not have enough time to devote to the Project and the planning of its associated activities. This funding is one way in which time can be provided.

A further point should be made about costs incurred by schools in our Project. In the twelve months, little use was made of outside providers to help with course provision. Teachers and members of the Project Team accepted responsibility for presenting programmes to staff. Or, in the case of one school, use was made of consultants from within the system. None of this input required payment. The Project thus showed the value of using skills that existed within a school. However, it can be anticipated that, as the action continues, schools will want to use other providers who will have to be paid for their services. It may be a little misleading to judge the costs on the basis of the limited expenses incurred in this Project. It can be concluded, however, that initiating programmes using a within-school development grant is highly feasible.

## Conclusion

The guidelines presented above were developed on the basis of experience in a year-long Project involving collaboration between three secondary schools and staff from a University School of Education. The Project was concerned with initiating action which would result in three secondary schools looking at their present situation to arrive at a set of priority needs which might be met through a programme of activities. That a needs survey would be carried out was to be accepted as part of the Project's demands on each school. In the broader context, however, there remains the question of how to persuade schools to undertake a review programme resulting in school-focused development activities. All three schools indicated that the Project represented a significant intervention. The programmes developed in each case attest to the strength of the impact of this intervention. But would a review programme have occurred in these schools if the Project had not been introduced?

The impetus for school-focused development programmes can come from two major sources. Action can be brought about either because of directives from without, that is, from school authorities or other groups such as a tertiary institution. Or the initiative can come from within, that is, from the staff of the school. Indications from the present study are that the latter will be rare. Teachers are busy teaching their classes, preparing students for public examinations, taking drama groups, training the choir, coaching sporting teams, participating in the activities of their professional association or the union, or just surviving day-to-day with school work. Reviewing general school developments does not have a high priority. It was not an insignificant reaction when the Project team was asked in each school either 'how much time will it all take?' or, 'will this mean I shall not get the chance to attend as many in-service courses which will keep me abreast of developments in my own subject teaching area?' These priorities, which were quite legitimate, were obvious to the University personnel.

There are serious implications here for school authorities anxious to instigate school improvement programmes. They have the task of persuading schools of the need for school review programmes and they must ensure that time can be set aside for the task. If it is left to schools to decide to take action, the indications from this Project are that usually very little will happen unless the Principal takes a more than active role. But it was not part of the brief for this Project to examine how authorities might generate school-focused in-service activities.

It became very clear to the Project team that teachers need to be convinced of the need for deliberate and reflective analysis of what is happening overall in the day-to-day activities of the school and what might happen. They also need to be convinced that external aid and support might help them to see matters from a different perspective, and overcome their insularity. Without the benefit of outside consultation there is the risk that schools will become totally inward looking and fail to see where change is needed. Teachers also need to be convinced that, as they review their school's situation, they are being asked to conduct an exercise which forms part of professional growth in the school rather than an exercise in deficiency analysis. The negative connotation associated with school 'needs' was very apparent in the interviews conducted in each school as part of the needs survey. All of this has implications for the way a Project of this kind might be initiated and sustained in a school.

A final point should also be made in relation to tertiary staff involvement in school-focused development programmes. If tertiary institutions are to become involved in this form of inservice activity (and the present Project demonstrated the value of such involvement), then decisions have to be taken which clarify the tertiary institution's attitude to the deployment of staff and resources as part of an expanded commitment to teacher education. Quite obviously, such decisions will involve consideration of working conditions as well as effective ways of coordinating demands on the institution. If such considerations do not take place, tertiary staff who decide to seek such involvement with schools may very quickly come to doubt the wisdom of their decision.

# References

AUCHMUTY, J.J. (Chairman) (1980) *Report of the National Inquiry into Teacher Education* Canberra, AGPS.

BAILEY, A.J. and BRAITHWAITE, R.J. (1980) 'Inservice education and the promotion of change in a secondary school' *British Journal of Teacher Education 6(3), 203–213.*

BAKER, K. and SIKORA, J.M. (1981) *The Schools and Inservice Teacher Education (SITE Evaluation Project 1978–1981. Final Report)* Bristol, School of Education, University of Bristol.

BATTEN, M. (1979) *Schools Commission Evaluation Studies. Report of a National Evaluation of the Development Program* Canberra, Schools Commission.

BENTZEN, M. (1974) *Changing Schools: The Magic Feather Principle* New York, McGraw Hill.

BOLAM, R. (1980) *Innovations in the Inservice Education and Training of Teachers. Final Synthesis Report on an OECD/CERI Project* Paris, OECD.

CORREY, P. (Chairman) (1980) *Teachers for Tomorrow. Continuity, Challenge* and *Change in Teacher Education in New South Wales* Sydney, Government Printer.

DAVIES, J.P. (1981) *The SITE Project in Northamptonshire 1978–1980. Final Evaluation Report* Mimeographed copy.

ELTIS, K.J., BRAITHWAITE, R.J., DEER, C.E. and KENSELL, H.G. (1981) *Fostering School-Focused Development Programs* Sydney, Macquarie University.

JAMES, Lord (Chairman) (1972) *Teacher Education and Training* (The James Report), London, HMSO.

KAHN, H. (1972) 'Teachers' centres as agencies for change' *Ideas* 23 October pp. 11–16.

SCHOOLS COMMISSION (1975) *Report for the Triennium 1976–78.* Canberra, AGPS.

SIEBER, S.D. (1981) Incentives and Disincentives for Knowledge Utilization in Public Education in LEHMING, R. and KANE, M. (Eds) *Improving Schools*, Beverly Hills, California, Sage.
TAYLOR, W. (1978) *Research and Reform in Teacher Education* Slough, NFER.

# School Reviews: A New Zealand Experience[*]

## Viviane M.J. Robinson
## University of Auckland, New Zealand

The last ten years have seen the emergence in OECD countries and in the United States of a new model of school improvement. The model is variously called 'in-school evaluation' (Shipman, 1979) 'school development' (Prebble and Stewart, 1981) or 'in-school reviews'. Under such a model, school staff themselves, rather than an external evaluator, are responsible for deciding what is to be evaluated, how it is to be evaluated and whether or not any changes are to be made as a result.

Until the emergence of the in-school review model, the predominant approach to school improvement has involved the management of innovations. Typically such innovations (like new maths or open-plan classrooms) are developed by outside specialists who consult in varying degrees with teachers and other interested groups. The process of school improvement then becomes one of disseminating information about the innovations and of persuading or regulating so that the maximum number of schools adopt them. There is a huge literature examining the characteristics of adopters and non-adopters, and the variables which influence whether or not, like grafted plants, the innovations 'take' in a particular school. The general consensus is that the management of innovation approach to school improvement has produced a few successes and a long line of resounding failures (Sarason, 1971; Whiteside, 1978). The shift from this model to a self-directed improvement process reflects both disillusionment with its results and a more positive desire to foster professional development and local initiative in schools.

[*] First published in *Education Management and Administration* 10 (1982) pp. 195–202. Reprinted with permission.

The purpose of this article is to elucidate some of the strengths and weaknesses of the school review model, as it was exemplified recently in New Zealand by the intermediate in-school reviews. First, I identify some of the assumptions about school development which were made by those who administered the reviews. Second, I compare these assumptions with the conclusions drawn by overseas researchers about how to promote effective school development. Third, I illustrate these points with qualitative data on the implementation of the reviews in three Auckland intermediate schools. Recommendations for the improvement of future reviews are made in the final section.

Departmental documents, correspondence and interviews with regional administrators provided information on the planning and coordination of reviews. At the school level, information was gained from relevant documents and from interviews with the principal and senior staff.

## Administration and Implementation of the Intermediate School Reviews

Between 1977 and 1980 New Zealand intermediate schools were invited by the Department of Education to take part in a voluntary self-evaluation exercise. By February 1981, forty-seven percent of the 142 intermediate schools in New Zealand had completed a review and it was unlikely that any more of them would do so. A departmental officer (Tate, 1978:7) defined the objectives of the review as:

> to help the intermediate schools to identify the needs of their pupils, to define their aims, to gather empirical data, to review their programmes and to evaluate their achievements; to help intermediate schools to become aware of alternatives and possibilities that may enable them to improve the quality of the education that they provide: to improve communication and cooperation between teachers, schools and parents, schools and the department

A national and district machinery was set up to help ensure the success of the reviews. A national consultative committee was charged with overseeing the progress of the reviews and making submissions to government on behalf of intermediate schools. The Minister of Education made two pupil-free days available to schools who submitted appropriate review plans to their regional authority.

At the district level, the inspector responsible for intermediate education established an advisory group to inform local principals about review procedures, and to provide resources such as information and teacher relief, to those schools who chose to take part (Tate, 1978: 9). In the Auckland region, the resource kit included background papers on intermediate education and a list of questions which could guide staff's information gathering activities. The questions were broad in scope and covered the following seven areas; the needs of children, guidance and counselling, evaluation and testing, curriculum, administration, community, and the local district. Most schools who completed a review surveyed at least one of these areas using procedures that ranged from informal staff discussion groups to formal questionnaires which were occasionally administered to pupils and parents as well as to staff. After reporting back at a series of staff meetings, a review report was written by either the principal or the leaders of review sub-groups. Occasionally, the school systematically followed up on a set of recommendations outlined in its report.

## Evaluation of the Implicit Review Model

Any attempt to foster self-evaluation or self-renewal in an organization rests on a set of assumptions about how to promote this activity. By identifying these assumptions I am not claiming that departmental officers and intermediate principals consciously set about producing a theory of school improvement. I am claiming, that by administering and implementing the review process in the way they did, they acted as if they believed the following to be true about school development.

1   *Voluntary involvement*   That staff that volunteer to do a review will be more committed and will generate more valid information about their school, than a staff which has been persuaded or coerced to do a review.

2   *Role of principal*   That the school principal should play a key role in deciding whether or not to conduct a review but should not direct or lead the review once a positive decision is made.

3   *Review method*
    i   That the conduct of a survey of one or more areas of a school's functioning is an appropriate method for fostering self-evaluation and self-improvement in school.

    ii  That school staff have sufficient technical skills to design, conduct and interpret the results of questionnaires and interviews administered to staff, parents and pupils.
    iii  That the interpersonal norms which exist in a staff group are supportive of problem-solving activities.

4  *Review outcomes*  That the process of conducting a review cannot be harmful to the school's current level of effectiveness. At worst, a review may have no impact on a school.

In short, it was assumed that school improvement could be accomplished by giving staff time off from teaching to systematically collect information which could be used to improve some aspects of the school's activity.

These assumptions are referred to collectively as the review model. To what extent does the model incorporate those features which research suggests are crucial to effective school development? What revisions to the model are suggested by this research and by the experiences of the three case-study schools?

### Voluntary involvement

Some recent literature on school development suggests that the desire to promote voluntary involvement was well founded. Where staff see participation as part of their professional development, projects are much more likely to be successful than where staff participate for political reasons, or because they are being paid to do so (McLaughlin and Marsh, 1978). But the issue of course is much more complex than just that of promoting a free and voluntary choice. Inspectors who believed that a review was worthwhile faced the following dilemma. If they strongly advocated the review, more schools might participate but there was an increased risk that they would take part for the wrong reasons. If they did not strongly advocate the review, fewer schools would take part but those that did would be more likely to be internally committed to the exercise.

More than two years after the start of reviews, one regional administrator still felt the dilemma: 'It's going to be necessary to put a bit of quiet pressure on them. But one minute I'm not supposed to pressure, and yet without it, they're letting it slide.'

Departmental officers in Auckland had attempted to resolve this dilemma by strongly advocating the idea of doing a review, without specifying how a particular school could benefit. This way of resolving the dilemma had two negative and unanticipated consequences. Firstly, if the inspector could not disclose why he thought a particular school should do a review, then he was powerless to challenge the principal's perceptions of its relevance to this school.

Secondly, despite an attempt to avoid applying pressure, some schools participated for the very reasons which the Department sought to discourage. Although principal B could not identify any problems in his school, he had nevertheless begun a review. He reported two reasons for doing so: 'The staff said, "Well, we'd better be in, or else we might get penalized." And secondly, I just put it to the staff when we were making a decision, that it would be a worthwhile experience just to see how much advantage would come out of it in comparison with our senior staff meetings, the agenda for which is very similar to much of what is in the review.'

The principal's perceptions of a trouble-free school are not challenged, nor are his staff's motives for participating. An opportunity for staff to identify and resolve some of their own concerns, is experienced by them like any other externally mandated school 'reform'.

## The role of the principal

The first assumption made about the role of the principal was that a review could not get started without the active interest and support of the principal. This assumption is widely supported in the school development literature. Fullan *et al* (1980) in their study of school development projects in the United States and Canada, reported that sixty-two per cent of their respondents perceived the commitment of their school administrators as crucial to getting the project started. The importance of a principal's commitment is also supported by the reviews of Spencer and Cullen (1978) and Runkel *et al* (1979). The second assumption, that is, that a principal should stay in the background while the review is conducted, is not consistent with the evidence. Verbal approval and encouragement to staff to 'go ahead', is not likely to produce a sustained and significant review exercise, since the review needs to be actively managed and have key school resources devoted to it (Nadler, 1981).

Interview data showed that the three principals played very different roles in their schools' review. Each of the three senior staff of school A, attributed the completion of their school's review to their principal.

> *Q:* Why did your school get through and complete its
> review?
> *Senior teacher:* Firstly, of course, the driving force was (the
> principal). If he starts something he sees it through.

For principal A, 'seeing it through' involved deciding on both the
type and membership of review groups, and making sure that
teachers had sufficient time to do a thorough job. In addition he
monitored both the pace and quality of the review activities: '. . . I
also asked people to think through their questionnaires. What
information did they want and what sorts of answers would people
give to their questions. . .? I was the coordinator of the exercise,
people kept me informed, I checked everything before it went out
and I set deadlines...'

In summary, principal A had seen his role as clearly advocating
the review to his staff, providing them with sufficient resources and
time to enable them to do a professional job and holding them
accountable for both the quality and pace of the review activities.

Principal B had also advocated the review to his staff, but he had
not identified any concerns or problems which a review might
address. The review was making slow progress and was limited in
scope. Several staff were not aware that it was occurring and others
may have been reluctant to commit time and effort to a project which,
according to the principal, was designed to compare the effectiveness
of a review with the effectiveness of the existing senior staff meetings.

In school C, the principal had discussed the possibility of doing a
review but many of his initially enthusiastic senior staff had since left.
He also reported that he was waiting for some of his new staff to
express enthusiasm about the review because they might then be
prepared to take on some of the hard work involved. A difficulty
with such a strategy, is that until they are confident of 'support from
the top', subordinates may not see it as in their professional self-
interest to become involved (Strauss, 1976).

## Review methods

This review model assumed that a survey of some or all aspects of a
school's functioning would be an appropriate method for school
renewal. It further assumed that school staff had both the technical
and interpersonal skills to collect data and to diagnose and discuss the
issues that may have been revealed by such a survey.

One of the biggest problems in any school development exercise is that of developing and sustaining staff's commitment. This is usually done by identifying a discrepancy between the current situation and an ideal or valued state. It is this awareness of falling short of one's own (individual or organizational) values that provides the motivation for a review exercise. The three case study schools undertook survey activities without previously identifying such discrepancies and although the review report was completed in school A, there was very little commitment to the process in schools B and C.

The survey approach created technical as well as motivational problems. Many staff expressed their frustration and their ignorance about the process of questionnaire construction. In school A a useful instrument was produced after weeks of painstaking experimentation and pilot-testing. Having gathered some data, staff faced further conceptual and theoretical difficulties with its interpretation.

The review model made no reference to the type of interpersonal behaviour and norms that are needed for a successful review. The resource material did not discuss the importance of norms which foster risk-taking, testing of assumptions, feedback and disclosure among the school's staff. Unless these norms are moderately or strongly established in a school (that is, there is already a climate in which problem-solving can occur), the problem identification and problem-solving functions will be restricted to those issues which can be resolved without violating important school values. An example from school B provides an illustration of how existing norms can restrict problem-solving activities. One of the items on a questionnaire to staff had asked: 'Do you think enough counselling assistance is available to staff?' Twelve people had said 'Yes' and eight people had said 'No'. A senior staff member reported the following reaction to these results: 'Twelve for 'Yes' and eight for 'No'. And yet when talking at senior staff level (in the senior administrative meeting), everybody felt that they couldn't understand why eight people should say that enough counselling wasn't available, when in actual fact, they are told at team meetings, and it's stated here over and over again, that if you've got a problem you should go to your team leader, or see the principal. So why eight of them should say 'No' is beyond me.'

The principal had previously reported in his interview that his school had very few problems and that any that arose were satisfactorily resolved in the senior staff meetings. The questionnaire however revealed a problem of which senior staff were unaware. Although the information had been collected about six months prior to the interview, it still had not been discussed with the respondents. Such discussion was reported to be ruled out by the fact that the questionnaires were confidential and anonymous.

The Department may have assumed, or hoped, that the potentially self sealing quality of the review process would be reduced if staff obtained information from such 'outsiders' as pupils, parents and community groups. But if school decision-makers cannot solicit, recognize and discuss negative feedback, then information from outsiders will be used to unilaterally confirm existing perceptions or to make only minor adjustments. In discussing the importance of surveying different interest-groups, principal B said: 'I would expect the staff's questionnaire to have the least possible bearing on any future changes. I would think that we'd get more suggestions from children to change, or from parents to change. But then by the same token, I qualify that remark by saying if I did expect a lot of change, then I would have heard from them by now surely.'

The same pattern of beliefs is evident in this discussion of parents' reactions to the school as was seen in the discussion of the staff's reaction. Inclusion of survey information from outsiders is no guarantee that the information will be used to 'test' the perceptions of insiders.

### Review outcomes

A final assumption incorporated in the review model concerned the impossibility of negative outcomes. Both departmental officers and senior teachers expressed the belief that at worst, the review would make no difference to the functioning of the school. Several school principals however, expressed the belief that while the review may have been a good experience, they would not do it again. The benefit the school gained was disproportionate to the amount of effort involved. This can be considered a negative or harmful result in the sense that they are expressing a cynicism or an unwillingness about 'incorporating the idea of a review and continuous self-evaluation into their programmes' (Tate, 1978: 8). Future suggestions about reviews, or curricular and administrative innovations may be met with attitudes of increased cynicism and decreased willingness to experiment.

In contracting with schools who were about to start a review, the Department did not require them to state the goals or anticipated outcomes of the exercise. Not only does this make any summative evaluation of the reviews difficult but there is some evidence that clear specification of the evaluation criteria during the contracting phase of a project is itself predictive of increased success (Havelock and Havelock, 1973). A few of the review reports, and the interview data from school A, suggest that the review produced changes in some aspects of the curriculum and in resource usage. There is scant data in the review reports about the level of commitment and interest of staff and few examples of crisis points, disagreements and surprising findings. In the absence of such careful qualitative data, it is difficult to tell how much impact the review has had on the communication, self-evaluative and problem-solving processes within the school.

## Summary and Recommendations

The intermediate in-school reviews was an early experiment in fostering self-evaluative and self-improvement processes in schools. This Chapter has suggested several ways in which the review model fell short of achieving its goals of school self-renewal. The first set of criticisms concerned the negotiation strategies used by the Department in obtaining the voluntary involvement of a school in a review. It was stressed that school staff cannot develop an internal commitment to a review unless they develop a clear sense of the specific problems that will be addressed. They also need to know how the suggested methods might help solve the problems and why those methods might be any more successful than those the school already uses. Such a negotiation process makes heavy demands on the skills of the review advocate. It requires both a clear understanding of organization development and the ability to both advocate and invite confrontation of one's views. These suggestions apply equally to the inspector, and to the principal who has become committed to the idea of a review and wishes to help his or her staff make a free and informed choice about their involvement.

The review model assumed that staff could identify and resolve important school problems with time off from teaching and some general guidelines about the types of question to ask. I have argued that this model is only helpful to staff who have already developed norms within their group that encourage sharing and testing of perceptions, openness between staff at different levels, and a willingness to experiment and take risks. In schools where there are numerous issues incapable of discussion, where staff are cynical about the probability of achieving change, and where upward communication flows are restricted, the model is unlikely to make an impact. In such cases, the self renewal activities of the school must be guided by an outsider who can by-pass the interpersonal and organizational games which prevent staff themselves from discussing important school problems. While such a consultant-guided intervention has the likely advantage of providing staff with a task-specific success in a relatively short time (Bassin and Gross, 1978) it may produce a continued dependence on consultant help. If this is a serious concern, then a subsequent contract should focus not on the task-related problem, but on the reasons why staff could not solve the problem for themselves. Such a contract involves a much more intensive, more time-consuming and more personally threatening exercise than the previous type (Argyris and Schon, 1978). This may be what is involved however, in becoming a self-renewing school.

## Note

The author thanks officers of the New Zealand Department of Education and the principals and senior staff of the three case study schools for their cooperation and criticisms of previous drafts of this chapter. The help of Chris Argyris, Tessa Blackstone, Christine Swarton and John Welton is also acknowledged.

## References

ARGYRIS, C. and SCHON, D. (1978) *Organizational Learning: A Theory of Action Perspective* Reading, Mass., Addison-Wesley.

BASSIN, M. and GROSS, T. (1978) Organization Development: A Viable Method of Change for Urban Secondary Schools. Paper presented to American Educational Review Association, Toronto, Ontario.

FULLAN, M., MILES, M.B. and TAYLOR, G. (1980) 'Organization development in schools: The state of the art' *Review of Educational Research* 50(1) pp. 121–83.

HAVELOCK, R.G. and HAVELOCK, M.C. (1973) *Training for Change Agents* Ann Arbor, Michigan: Center for Research on Utilization of Scientific Knowledge (CRUSK).

McLAUGHLIN, M.W. and MARSH, D.D. (1978) 'Staff development and school change' *Teachers College Record* 80(1) pp. 69–94.

NADLER, D.A. (1981) 'Managing organizational change: An integrative perspective' *Journal of Applied Behavioral Science* 17 pp. 191–211.

PREBBLE, T. and STEWART, D. (1981) *School Development: Strategies for*

*Effective Management* Palmerston, North, The Dunmore Press.

RUNKEL, P.J., SCHMUCK, R.A., ARENDS, J.H. and FRANCISCO, R.P. (1979) *Transforming the School's Capacity for Problem Solving*, Eugene, Oregon, CEPM.

SARASON, S.B. (1971) *The Culture of the School and the Problem of Change* Boston, Allyn and Bacon.

SHIPMAN, M. (1979) *In-school Evaluation* London, Heinemann.

SPENCER, L.M. and CULLEN, B.J. (1978) *Taxonomies of Organizational Change: Literature Review and Analysis*. Technical Report submitted to the U.S. Army Research Institute for the Behavioral and Social Sciences. Boston, McBer and Company.

STRAUSS, G. (1976) 'Organization development' in DUBIN, R. (Ed) *Handbook of Work, Organization and Society* Chicago, Rand McNally.

TATE, O. (1978) 'The intermediate education review' *Education* 27(5) pp. 7–9.

WHITESIDE, T. (1978) *The Sociology of Educational Innovation* London, Methuen.

# The Place of Organizational Development (OD) in Schools

## Philip J. Runkel and Richard A. Schmuck
## University of Oregon

A good deal of research has been done on the uses and effects of OD in schools (see for example, Schmuck and Miles 1971; Runkel and Schmuck 1977; Fullan *et al* 1980); the research provides evidence that OD can bring about sustained organizational change in schools. The major impact of OD lies in the socio-emotional domain where interventions can harmonize the interpersonal relations between teachers and students. In the more task-oriented improvements within organizations, changes in output, educational programming and structures are among the benefits of sustained OD. Interventions are more effective when the building administrator is supportive and when groups and subsystems are involved. In contrast to other approaches, the strategy of an OD consultant is to work with intact work groups so that the group itself, with group members helping one another, can make changes they desire in norms, procedure, organizational structure and interpersonal skill.

After combining the findings of a nation-wide survey in the US and Canada with other research, Fullan, Miles and Taylor (1980:176) wrote:

> OD seems beneficial to districts regardless of their size, wealth, location or socioeconomic character (but note the question of readiness criteria and the need for adaptation in urban settings). Districts that define their needs in task-oriented, educationally focused terms and consider structural changes a possibility are more likely to be successful ...

> OD programs have a favorable cost-benefit ratio: in many situations they can reasonably be expected to improve organizational climate and functioning, increase instructional in-

novations, and improve student outcomes. Dollar costs are often less than one-half of one percent of total budget ...

## Goals in OD

Typical goals for an OD programme of limited scope in school or district are: (a) to increase understanding of how personnel in different school jobs affect one another, (b) to develop clear communication networks up and down and laterally, (c) to increase understanding of the various educational goals in different functional parts of the school, (d) to uncover organizational conflicts for constructive problem-solving, (e) to develop new ways of solving problems through creative uses of new roles in groups, (f) to develop new ways of assessing progress toward educational goals in the school, (g) to involve more people at all levels in decision-making, or (h) to develop procedures for searching out innovative practices both within and outside the school. The overall or ultimate goal of OD is self-renewal, or institutionalizing a strong capacity for problem solving in the school or district. That capacity has been achieved only in a very few cases (see, for example, the descriptions of school K12 in Runkel, Wyant, Bell, and Runkel, 1980), but it remains the vision and the hope of many OD consultants. The concept has been discussed at length by Runkel, Schmuck, Arends, and Francisco (1979).

Far goals, however, are reached through small steps. In our work, we have usually used the following small steps as the primary ingredients of our OD strategy:

1   *Clarifying communication*   Clarity of communication is essential to any lasting organizational change. Members of the school must learn to clarify the communication they get from one another. Internal communication networks must operate at high fidelity, and external channels must map the environment accurately.

2   *Establishing goals*   Educational goals are usually ambiguous and diffuse. Organizational members can learn to clarify and share their objectives and to increase their sense of 'owning' the goals and integrating their efforts.

3   *Uncovering conflict and interdependence*   Clarifying communication processes and objectives will lead to increased awareness of conflict and interdependence. Confronting con-

flicts and exploring interdependence will help to establish norms and roles that will aid the school in accomplishing its educational tasks.

4 *Improving group procedures* Most organizational activity occurs in meetings of face-to-face groups. Meetings are rarely satisfying or productive for all faculty members; they are often frustrating. New skills for facilitating task productivity and group maintenance can help any meeting to be more satisfactory.

5 *Solving problems* Adaptability implies active engagement in continuous problem-solving cycles for identifying, analyzing, and acting on environmental contingencies. OD can help schools to extract creative solutions that yield a higher rate of success than solutions that merely extrapolate past practice.

6 *Making decisions* OD almost always disperses influence much more widely throughout the system than is usual in present day school organizations. Power need not be decreased in one job to be increased in another, although sometimes it is helpful to reduce authority if it is not based on knowledge and competence. Schools must learn alternative styles of making decisions to assure commitment from those who must carry out the decisions.

7 *Assessing change* Change for its own sake is not necessarily useful. Change should solve, or at least reduce problems. Schools must choose criteria for evaluating progress toward long-range and short-range goals.

## Meta-Skills

The seven steps or short-term goals listed just above constitute a very practical list. They are activities or skills that can be readily conceived and taught as skills in themselves. Indeed, they are headings of the core chapters in our Second Handbook (Schmuck, Runkel, Arends, and Arends, 1977). Nevertheless, each of those seven skills can be pulled apart to reveal smaller skills within it. For example, the skills of conducting productive meetings (No. 4 above) includes the skills of composing an agenda, keeping the discussion on the topic, checking the passage of time on each topic, making sure that each person has a clear chance to clarify his or her understanding of what others say, and so on. The skill of composing an agenda, in turn, includes finding out what topics members want to deal with the at the next meeting, getting them into an order reasonably satisfactory to participants, assigning an appropriate amount of time to each, and choosing people to introduce topics of which they have special knowledge or special concern. In brief, we could have made a much longer list of much smaller skills.

It is also possible to make a shorter list. Some skills useful in organizational life have the effect of sharpening the smaller skills, of maintaining their effectiveness. They are self-reflexive. They are skills through which a group or the school as a whole can watch how well it is applying the more detailed skills and, when necessary, take time out to improve the more detailed skills. In a recent book (see Chapter 4 of Runkel, Schmuck, Arends and Francisco, 1979), we called these watching-and-maximizing skills *meta-skills*. We described there four meta-skills that we believe to be of great aid in solving any problem. Beyond that, we believe they are essential to maintaining a strong capacity for solving problems in schools, whatever the problem, year in and year out. The four meta-skills are: (1) diagnosing the functioning of group and school, (2) gathering information and other resources from within and from outside, (3) mobilizing synergistic action, and (4) monitoring the other three meta-skills. A school with high levels of those skills, we believe, can deal productively with any difficulty whose chief sources do not lie outside the school's power to affect.

### Diagnosis

We mean by diagnosis the systematic inspection by school or subsystem of its own current functioning. We do not mean merely asking whether the group or school seems to be getting along with or without troubles. We mean asking whether what the group or school is doing matches the ways the members talk about what they are doing, and then whether what they are doing is what they want to be doing. We do not mean merely a yearly review – though that is usually a good idea – we mean to include formal and informal diagnosis as often as necessary to prevent radical, stressful reorganizations in response to crisis.

By systematic diagnosis, we mean two things, First, we mean collecting current data in a manner that will give answers in which one can have reasonable confidence. If information is sought about what frustrations people are feeling, for example, it will not do to ask only the principal, nor to ask faculty for oral statements at a faculty meeting. Methods are needed that will survey all the important segments of subsystem or school and that will enable respondents to feel safe in answering. We are talking about the kind of assessment that professional evaluators call formative evaluation – data to aid decisions about what to do next. This is not the place to go into technical detail. For advice on systematic diagnosis, see (among other sources) Chapter 2 of Schmuck, Runkel, Arends and Arends (1977).

Second, we mean using some sort of check list, written or mental, to make sure that some important aspect of organizational functioning is not forgotten – to suggest the kinds of inquiries a meta-skill in diagnosis might prompt problem solvers to undertake. The particular list used is not as important as having one, as long as it does in fact remind the user of the important features of organizational life. The seven skills we listed earlier could serve as a check list.

### Gathering Information and Other Resources

By searching for information and other resources, we mean initiating searches from within or from outside school or group whenever the present information or other resources seem inadequate to plan an effective solution to a problem. A mundane example occurs not rarely in a problem-solving group that plans a solution requiring money to buy certain materials. An uncertainty then arises whether the principal has the necessary money or can get it, and then whether the principal will be willing to allocate it for the groups' purpose. It is not rare that a group will say, 'I think she will give us the money', more on the basis of hope than on the basis of any evidence for thinking so. Some will urge going ahead with the plans on the supposition that the principal will give the money, despite the lack of any information to support the supposition. Some will recommend giving up the project on the supposition that the principal will not give the money, despite the lack of any information to support the supposition. Some, at last, will urge asking the principal whether she can disperse money for the materials.

Those varieties of response to uncertainty are common in group meetings at all levels of schools and districts (and in other kinds of organizations, for that matter). A group skilful in dealing with problems will assess the degree to which later action depends on resolving an uncertainty. ('Do we need to know what might happen at that juncture?') If the possible answers to an uncertainty will have little effect on further action, the skilful group drops the discussion. If the answers to the uncertainty can make a difference, the skilful group decides when the uncertainty must be resolved, how to get information to resolve it, and who will take the necessary steps. Those are the components of searching out information and resources.

Skill in getting information and other resources is obviously important to solving problems. A solution to a problem can founder if it turns out that participants have less than they need of information, status, affection, services, materials or money.

### *Mobilizing Synergistic Action*

Even if a school were to exhibit well developed norms, structures and procedures for systematic diagnosis and for getting information and resources from inside and outside, we would still not predict it to show an exemplary capacity for solving problems. Even when an accurate diagnosis of the present situation has been agreed upon by all concerned, when a clear and specific target has been consensually chosen, and when people have declared their commitment to realistic and well understood steps of action, even then a crucial step remains. Someone must actually take the first, risky, irretrievable action in the new mode. That first step into action is usually a very big one for participants in change. We have seen many groups able to do excellent planning but unable to act on the plans.

We emphasize the necessity for synergistic group action in organizational change, because new norms and role-relationships are more than the sum of individual actions. Administrators and others too often try to bring about an organizational change by instructing every individual what to do and then saying, in effect, 'On next Monday morning, do things the new way, not the old way'. As everyone except top administrators seems to know, that method often puts people in a very risky situation. They may have little confidence that they can do the new thing correctly – in a manner that will please, or at least not draw the wrath, of all the others involved in the change. It is often safer to go on doing things the old way. (They can always claim they didn't understand the instructions.)

If change is to proceed to a new pattern of stability, members must be in frequent communication up, down, and laterally to keep up with every latest development. Collaboration must replace isolation and hierarchical direction so that commitment to new action can be accurately ascertained and adequately supported. With intimate collaboration in processing problems and making decisions, new patterns of coordinated action can take forms that cannot possibly be brought into being by directives to separate individuals.

A strongly cohesive group in which members share understandings of their purposes, norms, skill and resources, in which those understandings are both explicit and intuitive and in which every member confidently expects other members to act so as to support his or her own acts – such a group can achieve results that cannot be achieved by individuals directed from above. So far as we know, no basketball coach has ever expected to win a game by sending a memorandum of instructions to each player, ending with, 'Go out there Monday night and do it'.

### Monitoring the First Three Meta-Skills

Monitoring the first three meta-skills is the crowning skill necessary to sustaining a capacity for solving problems in the school. It is the skill of being able to observe one's own group and ask, 'Are we as skilful as we need to be in diagnosing our functioning, getting appropriate information and resources, and mobilizing our action synergistically? Are we able to move ourselves in the directions we want to go?' Answering those questions gives the group or school an awareness of its capacity to deal with problems productively.

When a group or school is aware of its problem-processing capacity, it does not examine its meta-skills in a vacuum. It examines them in the context of the content-problems it has been trying to alleviate. It will be able to describe its own norms, structures, and procedures. It will examine goals, plans and actions and question their relevance. It will display upshifting: it will ask not merely whether it is achieving its goals; it will also ask whether the goals are worth achieving.

A mature meta-skill is of course institutionalized. It is maintained through norms, structures and procedures. A school that wishes to sustain a lively capacity for solving problems will review its meta-skills periodically. It will assign that duty to a particular subsystem to be sure it gets done, but of course it will welcome assessments from any individual at anytime.

### Sequences in OD

Sequencing of activities in an OD programme is very important. No single sequence is suitable to every school, but some things are better done before other things. We have discussed sequencing in some detail in Chapter nine and ten of Schmuck, Runkel, Arends, and Arends (1977) and in Chapter five of Runkel, Schmuck, Arends, and Francisco (1979). Briefly, however, the main parts of an OD programme usually go in this order:

1 Initial contact with the administrator and the board of education to gain general approval for the intervention.

2 Commitment from the entire faculty about the intervention. During discussions with the faculty agreements are made about goals, time and energy; the consultant makes clear that he or she is consultant to the entire faculty, not just to one segment of it such as the administration.

3 Data-gathering concerning existing organizational processes of the school.

4 Feedback of data to the target school.

5 Establishment of the specific goals of the OD intervention for this faculty.

6 Carrying out a training programme.

7 Data-gathering to ascertain effects of the training while it is proceeding. Decisions about termination are guided by these data and made jointly between the consultants and the participants.

The training programme, listed as No. 6 above, is made up of certain skills, exercises, and procedures that together form the building blocks of OD technology. The term *skill* signifies a way that certain interactions with others can be executed in a group. Sometimes the skill is one of communication, such as paraphrasing what another has said so that the other can verify whether he has been understood. Sometimes it is a skill of the group convener, such as guiding a group through a survey of opinion. Sometimes the skill involves writing interview schedules to obtain diagnostic information about a school.

The skills practised during OD interventions are put to work only in reciprocal relations between persons; no individual can make use of these skills in isolation. Each skill is actually one person's part of a reciprocal role-relation. Paraphrasing, for example, can only be done in conversation with at least one other person; it is not a complete act until the other has verified the accuracy of the paraphrase. The skill of a pair or group, consequently, is often surprisingly independent of the presumed skill of the individuals composing it. The convener can be skilful in conducting a survey only if the members know their parts of the role-relation; an interview schedule can be prepared effectively only if the interviewers using the schedule act with the same goals and values as the writer and only if the respondents join the communicative act in the way the writer and the interviewer anticipate.

We draw a distinction in OD training between exercises and procedures. An exercise is a game that participants are asked to play to teach them something very important about group dynamics. Participants are able to understand the important principle about the group process because they have just experienced the principle through their own behaviour.

A procedure refers to an interpersonal form for communication in a group that helps the group to complete a task. A procedure can be used for a variety of tasks or purposes. Another would be the theatre-in-the-round procedure for sharing ideas and making observations.

## Providing Consultants

Lists of competent OD consultants can be obtained from Certified Consultants International (PO Box 574, Brentwood, Tennessee, USA, 37027), The National Training Laboratories (PO Box 9155, Rosslyn Station, Arlington, Virginia, USA, 22209), and the Center for Educational Policy and Management (College of Education, University of Oregon, Eugene, Oregon, USA, 97403). They can be useful whenever a school or district undertakes a change that affects roles and interpersonal relationships. We think the best use a school district can make of OD consultants, however, is to engage them to teach selected members of the school district to act as OD consultants within their own district. That is, we believe that the most cost-effective way to provide a continuing capacity for problem solving is to form a group of members of the district who can be called upon by any part of the district to provide OD consultation. Several districts in the US and Canada now have such cadres. The features of those 'cadres of organizational specialists', as we call them are given on page 183 of this book. The story of the formation of the first such cadre has been written by Runkel, Wyant, Bell, and Runkel (1980).

## What OD Does

OD does not tell you how best to teach, though it may offer you some ways of altering the group dynamics in your classroom. OD does not tell you how best to keep financial records, though it may offer you some ways to help members of the district understand better the meaning and implications of the figures you write down. OD does not tell you how to schedule classes, though it may alert you to some deeper effects of your scheduling on the image of the school held by teachers and students. OD does not tell you how to design schoolbuildings, though it may remind you of some patterns of communication that you might want the architecture to enhance. In sum, OD consultants, in that role, are not experts in the immediate content or task at hand. They do not come into the school presuming to know what is best for the school.

OD facilitates. OD consultants try to increase the clarity with which school people choose what they want to do, the steps through which they do it, and the signs by which they can decide whether they have succeeded. OD consultants help school people to visualize the interpersonal and organizational procedures that will help and those that will hinder. They help school people to bring into legitimate concern any opinion or feeling that can affect the job at hand, including conflicts between factions and strong emotions. They offer ways the members of the school can make productive use of conflicts and emotions that are ordinarily suppressed.

Above all, OD consultants teach participants how to be helpful to their colleagues in the ways the consultants themselves are helpful. OD consultants do not try to make their craft esoteric and secret. They try to make it as clear, simple, and learnable as possible. They try to leave the school, in brief, with a higher level of meta-skill, a higher organizational capacity for solving any kind of problem, than when they came in.

## References

FULLAN, M., MILES, M.B. and TAYLOR, G. (1980) 'OD in schools: The state of the art' *Review of Educational Research* 50(1) pp. 121–183.

RUNKEL, P.J. and SCHMUCK, R.A. (1977) 'Review of research findings' in SCHMUCK, R.A., RUNKEL, P.J., ARENDS, J.H. and ARENDS, R.I. (Eds) *Second Handbook of Organization Development in Schools* Palo Alto, CA, Mayfield, pp. 33–38.

RUNKEL, P.J., SCHMUCK, R.A., ARENDS, J.H. and FRANCISCO, R.P. (1979) *Transforming the School's Capacity for Problem Solving* Eugene, Oregon, Center for Educational Policy and Management.

RUNKEL, P.J., WYANT, S.H., BELL, W.E. and RUNKEL, M. (1980) *Organizational Renewal in a School District: Self-Help Through a Cadre of Organizational Specialists* Eugene, Oregon, Center for Educational Policy and Management.

SCHMUCK, R.A. and MILES, M.B. (Eds) (1971) *Organization Development in Schools* La Jolla, CA, University Associates.

SCHMUCK, R.A., RUNKEL, P.J., ARENDS, J.H. and ARENDS, R.I. (1977) *Second Handbook of Organization Development in Schools* Palo Alto, CA, Mayfield.

*Section Four:*
# A Call to Action

---

*The two chapters in this final section constitute a call to action. The authors take the themes implicit in the book and consider how they can be made manifest in schools and in local situations.* **Philip Runkel** *discusses how we might improve our adaptability (and that of our schools), and turns to biological diversity for an analogy.* **Marvin Wideen** *and* **Ian Andrews** *take a practical approach by developing some of the underlying themes and issues in the book into principles that can guide school improvement efforts in local settings. These two chapters take as their broad aim (as do the other contributions to this book), the improvement of schooling: to make schools better places in which we and our children can act out our lives.*

# Maintaining Diversity in Schools

Philip J. Runkel
University of Oregon

All the contributors to this book have touched upon diversity in one way or another. Richard Schmuck maintained that an autonomous school could be so only if it developed its own unique way of doing things – if it appreciated its difference from other schools. When David Hopkins discussed the inevitability of incremental change, I think he was seeing the diversity of people in schools, the diversity of the environments of schools, and the difficulty of predicting the effects of those diversities as changes move along and have their own effects. Bruce Joyce writes about the ways diverse people and schools react to proposals for new curricula or to proposals for in-service education and the ways they can adapt them to their own uniqueness. In calling the teacher an artist, Lawrence Stenhouse reminded us again of the uniqueness of every teacher's teaching. Stenhouse also urged teachers and schools to be experimental; to make use of the diverse capabilities within themselves. And Jean Rudduck said that every unique teacher must deal with a unique community of students. All these people, I believe, conceive uniqueness and diversity as inevitable and even as sources of opportunity.

## Change

It is often said that we must live nowadays with rapid change. It is said just as often that the more things change, the more they stay the same. In the case of schools, we can put those two statements together by saying that many schools are trying many new things nowadays, but when we go back a year or two after a new thing has been identified, we see little or no evidence of it remaining.

Why do schools keep trying new things if the trials result mostly in one failure after another? I think two reasons account for most of the continuing effort. The first reason is that administrators receive praise from colleagues, from superintendents, from school board members, and even from some parents for putting on a show of trying to make schools better in some way. Sometimes they even get raises in salary, and sometimes they even get hired into better jobs. In short, being innovative is a way for school administrators to advance their careers.

The second reason is that many people honestly believe that schools should be improved in some way – that schools too often mislead students about the nature of the world they are growing into, that schools impart knowledge but fail to teach students how to apply the knowledge outside of school, that schools fail to put their greatest effort on the most important things for students to learn, and so on. I don't see any consensus on those questions. Administrators, teachers, parents, legislators, children, professors of education – no group agrees very well with another about what 'good' schools should look like, nor do people within any one group agree very well with one another. But many people in all those groups want the schools changed somehow.

The demand for change spurs not only administrators to innovate, but also many others connected with schools. Some parents band together to demand back-to-basics. Some students band together to demand greater 'relevance'. Some professors quote each other in demanding more 'affective' education. And so on.

But why do those groups go on making those demands in the face of the many efforts to do those things that fail? One reason, of course, is that not many people know how to judge whether a thing has succeeded or failed. Many people do not even ask for a systematic assessment of outcomes to be made. They simply take it for granted that if the school announces a programme of 'basic education', for example, that the students are indeed getting what they suppose those words stand for.

There is another reason – an important one. I think Lawrence Stenhouse and Ted Aoki and Karl Weick (1979: 246–249, 261–263) would say that what looks like failure to an accountant or an expert in MBO can look like liveliness and experimentation and appropriate variation to others; a way of doing things that is suitable for another year, another teacher, or another group of students. Relinquishing that way of doing things may not signal failure; it may signal alertness to current needs. I agree. Indeed, I shall return to that point later. And I suppose there are still other reasons that people go on wanting to change things. But I leave the other reasons to Sigmund Freud.

The demand for change seems to me reasonable and sound. I agree with the people who say that schools must respond better (somehow) to the changes going on in society. But I disagree with the people who want to pick out certain feature of the modern world and then make sure that all schools prepare students to cope with those features. I disagree because those features may be the wrong ones, and also because those features may no longer be there by the time the students are in a position to cope with them. I also disagree with the people who hope to cope with our changing world by teaching each individual student how to be adaptable. I disagree because humans are social creatures. Their individual ability to adapt to their environment is useless without their social ability to adapt – their ability to adapt as cooperative groups and collectivities.

## Current Trends in Society and Culture

I suppose I ought to say a few words about the idea that our world is changing radically. I mean, for example, that the energy shortage will become very severe. The shortage of oil will cause shortages in food, clothing, medicines, building materials, and in the distribution of everything. The energy shortage and inflation, together, will increase the conflict and the enmity between the haves and the have-nots. Continuing rising expectations will widen the gap. The effects will show both between classes within nations and between nations. Racism, nationalism, and other forms of ethnocentrism will combine with economic disparities to exacerbate the enmity. Military actions are likely to increase.

At the same time that those economic strains will increase the conflict between groups and between nations, strains in social control will increase. Two trends in social control are now in conflict; those trends are centralization and self-management. On the one hand, the central governments of nations continue to grow, providing more and more services (or trying to) and imposing more and more regulations. Computer technology has so far spurred centralization, not lessened it. On the other hand, there is now a movement toward local self-management in all parts of the world. It takes many forms: nationalism, resentment and distrust of 'big government', local business cooperatives, communes, counter-cultures, refusal of government aid by local groups, family farms, the conservative yearning for a return to free enterprise, the resentment of taxes for welfare, and the growth of the underground economy. It even appears in the literature on educational research; namely, in the finding that educational innovation doesn't work unless the people in the local school modify the innovation to make it their own unique thing. [A great deal of writing has appeared about the trends I have set forth, but little has yet appeared about the ways schools will be affected. I leave the effects on schools as an exercise for the reader. Here is a sampling of literature on the trends I have mentioned: Alschuler *et al* (1977), Anderson (1976), Appley and Winder (1977), Argyris and Schon (1974), Bowles and Gintis (1976), Coleman (1972), Davis and Cherns (1975), Deci (1972), Elgin and Bushnell (1977), Elgin and Mitchell (1977), Freire (1972), Hedberg, Nystrom, and Starbuck (1976), Hespe and Wall (1976), ISR Newsletter (1977), Kaufman (1979), Meyer and Rowan (1977), Schumacher (1979), Smith (1976), Stavrianos (1976), Slobaugh and Yergin (1979), Weizenbaum (1976), Zwerdling (1979).] The conflict between centralization and decentralization will complicate the conflicts over ways to resolve all the other conflicts.

## Adaptability

We are facing, it seems to me, an unprecedented series of demands upon our adaptability. By adaptability, I mean simply coping with change effectively enough to maintain continuity in our technological civilization. When I say continuity, I do not mean that our civilization must be maintained in its present form; indeed, I believe it cannot be. I mean only that I would like to see the changes made in a way that does not fragment our civilization into a hodge-podge of warring groups.

My fear may seem extreme. But the demands for change that will soon be upon us are unprecedented in the geographical compass of the economic stresses, the rapidity with which they will tumble one upon the heels of the last, the depth with which they will penetrate all sectors of every nation, and the compression of the time we shall have to cope with them adequately.

By adaptability of schools, I mean the corresponding thing – coping with change effectively enough to maintain continuity of some sort of schooling for a reasonably predictable body of students in a locality, and doing so in a way that does not result in a hodge-podge of warring groups among faculty, parents, administrators, students, and employers. Even if you do not share my fear of the extremes, I hope you will grant that the adaptability of schools is going to be more severely tested in North America and in Western civilization generally than ever in the past.

How can we be ready for the changes? That is, how can we make sure that our adaptability is lively enough to cope with the changes? For answers to those questions, I turn to genetic adaptability and then draw the analogy to organizational life.

## The Gene Pool

With the possible exception of the insects, humans are the most adaptable species on the earth. Like the insects, we have spread around the globe into the driest deserts, into the rainiest tropics, and almost from pole to pole. We have put towns two miles above sea level and sent explorers a mile below sea level. Going beyond the insects, we are sending explorers into airless space.

Our inventiveness and our social adaptability rest on our biological adaptability. Like that of most species on earth, our adaptability rests on the vast variety of the assortment of genes with which individuals can be endowed and upon the gene pool in the population from which an individual's genes can be drawn. Because of the essentially random reassortment of genes (and their variants called alleles) every time a sperm meets an ovum, different individuals have very different propensities for dealing with the environment. Given the same diet, some of us put on fat much more rapidly than others. Given the same concentration of bacteria or automobile fumes, some of us get sick more quickly than others. Given the same kind of psychological threat, some of us get more anxious than others. And so on. Despite the fact that we can rarely calibrate the ways that one genetic endowment or another makes use of experience or training, there is no doubt that we come into the world with different capacities – methods, so to speak – of dealing with our environment.

Our differences do not protect individuals from environmental stresses, but they protect humankind as a whole from them. Our species survives despite the fact that catastrophes kill off great numbers of individuals. The terrible bubonic plague in the middle ages in Europe killed off only a quarter of the population.

Under certain circumstances, some of our capacities seem to be debilities. To put on fat in the tropics seems a disadvantage, but to put on fat in cold climates seems an advantage. At first glance, sickle-cell anaemia seems something none of us would want to have, but people who carry the heterozygotic gene that makes them susceptible to anaemia are also resistent to malaria. If you are surrounded with malaria-bearing mosquitos and want to go on living, sickle-cell anaemia is a good thing to have.

So far, I have described two important features of biological adaptability: (1) The great variety among individuals provides insurance for the population against stress from the environment. If all the individuals were alike, some stress might come along that would destroy them all. Since they have different ways of reacting to environmental stress, no particular stress kills them all – the population survives; (2) A characteristic that looks to us like a debility, like something undesirable, may be very desirable at a deeper level. Since we do not know against what threats some of our seeming debilities may protect us in the future, we bring unknown dangers upon ourselves when we try to eradicate what seems now to be an annoying, painful, or debilitating characteristic. Paul Ehrlich (1979) mentions that years ago, a strain of wheat was developed that is superbly adapted to the climate and to the insect and fugus populations in Turkey. Now, all the wheat farmers in Turkey grow that one strain. When some insect or fungus comes along that can attack that strain, all Turkey, in one season, will be without wheat.

Now I turn to the four features that Walter Buckley (1967) specifies for an adaptive system, whether the system is a human individual, an organization, or humankind as a whole.

The first is continuing interaction with the environment. Individuals and their collectivities are open systems, of course, and therefore they must interact with the environment to stay alive – they must breathe the air, for example, every few seconds. But Buckley means that we must act on our environment as well as being acted upon by it if we are to remain adaptable. We must continually sample the varieties of interaction that our environment offers us. Biologically, the varieties of genetic endowment in a population enable a great variety of ways of dealing with the environment to go on at the same time within the population. Socially and culturally, we need to maintain interaction with a variety of other cultures if we are to remain flexible. When a people stays isolated too long, its adaptability becomes fragile. The Native Americans in North America and the aborigines in Australia, among others, give us examples of cultures that were violently disrupted and almost destroyed by being thrust suddenly into interaction with a culture very different from their own. I think there is reason to worry that Western civilization as a whole is reaching that same fragility, simple because it has become so powerful and so widespread that it can ignore – temporarily – other cultures.

Buckley's second feature of an adaptive system is its pool of variety or diversity. As I said earlier, a population maintains genetic variety through the recombination of genes in its offspring. I shall speak later of what we might mean by a pool of variety in schools.

Buckley's third feature is selection; that is, some mechanism through which the potentially available ways of doing things can be sifted and a selection can be made of the ways of doing things best suited to immediate problems. That is done biologically through natural selection, a process by which, through sexual reproduction, certain characters or ways of doing things in a present environment become more widely represented among the individuals in the population. Socially, culture serves the same purpose. Cultures specify certain ways of doing things. The ways differ from environment to environment over the face of the earth. In some ways, culture seems to work faster than heredity, and in other ways slower.

Buckley's fourth feature is some way to preserve the 'successful' ways of doing things in the population. Biologically, genes are preserved because they are passed on to offsprings. Even though a particular gene or allele may become sparse or recessive in a population, it is very unlikely to vanish entirely. (I cannot explain the reason for that, because I am not well enough versed in the arithmetic of genetics). The only thing that interferes with the process I have just described is mutation. We might call mutation the mechanism of replenishing the variety pool that evolution falls back on when all else fails.

## Social Adaptation

Now we come to the matter of drawing a parallel between genetic adaptability and social adaptability. Just as we can ask how a population of biological organisms maintains diversity and adaptability, so we can ask how a population of human organizations – like schools – maintains diversity and adaptability. It has often happened in the past that a biological species failed to maintain sufficient adaptability and vanished from the face of the earth. Perhaps the same thing happens to our human organizations, though the mechanisms must be somewhat different, since as long as there are humans, there is bound to be some sort of human organization.

But it does not go without saying that there must always be some sort of school. There must always be some sort of teaching and learning, I am sure, but I don't think there must forever be schools. I don't think schools are part of our biological inheritance. Presumably there was a time when there weren't any schools. My concern, if schools must change, is that they change with some reasonable continuity, doing so in a way that is not cataclysmic, doing so in a way that does not result in a hodge-podge of warring groups.

Through some magical arithmetic of my own, I shall now use the two points I made earlier and the four points I took from Buckley and state five things we must do if we want to improve the adaptability of our schools.

## Five Things To Do

1 *Deliberately maintain diversity (variety) in the way we do things, anything and everything, in schools.* (This is my point 1 above.) Do it as insurance against change, in the same way you take out insurance against windstorms and fire. Do it because we cannot know what new ways of doing things we shall need in the future – even tomorrow.

2 *Maintain the pool of variety by maintaining actual deviant practices.* (This is a combination of Buckley's points 2 and 4.) Bruce Joyce said this, too. It is not sufficient to have descriptions or practices in a file or in the library. When a new problem arises, our natural tendency is to turn first to some way of coping with it that we already have had some experience with or at least have seen someone else use. If the practice is already in being, we have some confidence that it will 'work'.

Starting with the printed word to bring a new practice into being is much more chancy – or at least it feels like it to most people. For one thing, we can see too many places where something could go wrong. For another thing, merely finding the right article or book can be an immense task in itself. I am not saying we should do away with libraries, archives, or (in the US) the Educational Resources Information Center (ERIC). I am only saying that relying on repositories of print alone is like relying on antiquarians to tell us how to cope with new problems. But I need not belabour the point; everyone is now familiar with the inadequacies of the printed page to spur innovation.

The National Diffusion Network (NDN) in the United States, by the way, is a reasonably successful example of a way to use persons who travel from place to place to increase the tangibility of new ways of doing things. The travellers of the NDN can bring together printed descriptions of ways of doing things, groups who have actually done things that way, and schools looking for new ways of doing things.

Diversity can be maintained in being by permitting and encouraging persons and groups to do something differently. Current examples are alternative schools, a group of teachers in a school teaching as a team while others do not, different modes of making decisions in different schools, different scheduling patterns in different schools, different ages for compulsory attendance in different provinces, and different teachers in a school using different teaching methods. I believe it is urgent that we push diversity well beyond those examples.

**3** *Establish a conscious way of selecting the most suitable ideas for use in dealing with current problems.* (This is Buckley's point 3.) In most schools and districts, there is not a specified and commonly understood procedure for deciding when a problem warrants doing something special about it, nor for deciding just what to do about it. (See Chapter two of Runkel, Schmuck, Arends, and Francisco, 1979, for a discussion of selecting certain difficulties to be treated as problems.) The result of that lack of procedure is that some important problems go unrecognized, some problems are worked on by several persons or groups unbeknown to one another, and the resources brought to bear on problems are often fewer than they could be.

In some schools, the job of selecting problems is given over to the principal (and in a district to the superintendent), often more by default than by plan. In others, certain problems are selected by the curriculum committee, others by the discipline committee, and so on. But even in schools where certain persons or committees are charged with keeping an eye out for certain kinds of problems, their procedures usually remain fortuitous, haphazard, and uninspected. It is possible, in contrast, for the person or committee to set up a conscious procedure for reviewing the procedures by which problems are brought to attention and chosen for special action.

Difficulties are converted into problems not only by persons or committees sitting and thinking about the matter. Problems are also thrust upon the school by parents and other interest groups, by formal evaluations, by mandated programmes from provincial and national governments, by heavy snowstorms, by the discovery of poisonous materials in the building, by changes in the student population, and by a thousand other sources. Putting priorities on all those possible problems and choosing the best ways of alleviating them can become a gargantuan task.

You might say that one way to maintain variety is to maintain at least some schools where selecting problems and methods of dealing with them is done, indeed, in a haphazard manner. I will accept that idea if the school includes a periodic review of its effectiveness in dealing with problems. It should ask itself whether it chose the best problems and the best solutions during the past year and whether it wants to go on using a haphazard method.

**4** *Build channels to more parts of the social environment through which information and influence can reach the school.* (This is Buckley's point 1.) Schools (at least those in the US) have long responded mostly to white, middle-class, male, English-speaking ways of doing things. There are other varieties, and rich varieties, of ways to do things in those minority sectors of society that the dominant class has so long treated as aberrations and embarrassments. Perhaps the recent trend (I think there is a trend) toward pluralism and toward respect for ethnic and local sub-cultures will increase the access of the dominant class to the diversity residing in those sectors.

**5** *Accept the discomfort, anxiety, and even fear that comes from harbouring deviance.* (This is my point 2 above.) Accept it as the price of maintaining adaptability – the price of insurance against catastrophic change. Accept the fact that there is more than one good way to do something. Accept the fact that today's good way may be tomorrow's bad way.

If someone else is doing something in a way different from the way we are doing it, we often interpret that fact as a criticism. 'They think they are better than we are,' we say. That reaction is common in schools when one group of teachers undertakes an innovation of some sort. It is common among principals when one of them tries something new. And so on. That reaction rests on the assumption that there must be one best way of doing something – that one way must be better than another. If we are to maintain variety, we must come to see that what is good for one place or one person or one time is not necessarily good for another.

Different ways of doing things can be threatening, too, because the mere existence of the other way can make us worry whether we are doing as well as we ought – whether we ought to be doing it that way. We must not only accept the difference of other people from us, but also the difference of our ourselves from them.

We can also worry that other ways of doing things will directly and actively interfere with our own ways of doing things. If one student in a class speaks in a very loud voice, the teacher can worry that all the other students will begin speaking in very loud voices. Then the teacher will have to do so, the teacher across the hall will hear the unusual volume of sound and talk about it to other teachers, and a hundred other bad things will happen. But it is also possible that the class can learn to let the one student have his or her own mannerisms.

That is the end of my list of things to do to promote and maintain diversity.

## Present Diversity

I have given some examples of groups and activities that encourage or maintain diversity. In other words, people are already doing something about it. So why am I taking the trouble to say all this? I'm sure you know the answer. I don't think the present diversity is sufficient to give us adequate insurance against the future.

Despite the considerable amount of innovation going on in schools, they seem to me to remain remarkably uniform. As I travel from school to school, I see that schooling goes on in school buildings and not elsewhere. I know what kinds of rooms and what kinds of arrangements of them I'll encounter. I know that the principal will have an office of his or her own, and the teachers won't. I know the hours during the day that the buildings will be occupied and empty. I know that I'll find the students in the rooms except when they are moving quickly to other rooms. I know that every room will have a 'front', and the teacher will be standing there. I know that the students will be clustered and segregated by age. I know that students of a certain age will be studying about the same sort of thing, taught by about the same methods and often out of the same or very similar books, from school to school and city to city. I know that the students will be given grades and that the criteria for the grades will be about the same everyplace. And so on.

I know that I am exaggerating a little. You will already be saying to yourself that you know a school where something I have said is not true. I don't doubt it. So do I. I can name many schools where something recognizably different is going on. I can even name a few schools where something radical is going on. Nevertheless, I cannot think of a single school where things were so different that I was confused about what room to hunt for, to whom to speak about what, and what questions to ask to understand what the school was doing. I would like to see a school that plunged me into that kind of confusion.

I also worry about the fact that the more things change, the more they stay the same. It is true that many schools are trying new things. It is also true that most of those new things soon fade away, and things go back to normal. It has almost come to the point where, when we speak of an innovative school, we mean one that tries one new thing after another without making any of them work.

But perhaps my worry is misplaced. Perhaps that constant toying with new ways of doing things is a way of maintaining diversity in being. Maybe those innovative schools provide the pool of variety from which we can draw new ideas when we need them. We can go to McKenzie School this year to see team teaching in operation, and if McKenzie School drops team teaching after this year, we can see it next year in Fraser School.

I am sure that the rotation of different innovations in schools is, indeed, one of the ways we maintain diversity in being. But there are two things I don't like about that method. The first is that it gives us a collection of examples of things that do not work. Maybe those things could work, but we can't see very well how to make them work if all our examples are failures – if we call them failures. When considering an innovation that was tried elsewhere, it is too easy to say, rhetorically, 'It didn't work for them; why should it work for us?'

The other thing I don't like about the rotation method is that it is too costly. Change always requires more energy than routine does. If a school spends energy beyond its budget for a year or two and then finds itself no better off than before, the costs are serious. First, the regular programme will inevitably have suffered some neglect in the hope that the new thing would compensate. Second, the school will have lost what it might have gained had it chosen a more suitable innovation. And third, the prognosis for any attempt at innovation in the near future will have worsened, since a 'failure' always weakens confidence in the possible benefits of the next innovative effort. The amount of energy and enthusiasm that is nowadays draining away from teachers into aborted innovation is frightful.

I would like schools to be allowed the time, and be given the resources, to work long and hard at a new idea and make it work. I would like one school in a region to stand for some years as the place you go to see one alternative way of doing something, and see it working, another to stand as the place where you see another alternative working, and so on. I would like each school to be proud to display their kind of thing without feeling either superior or inferior to other schools.

Perhaps I should say something here about the survival of the fittest. Some people sometimes use that phrase to oversimplify matters. Evolutionary adaptation works to increase the likelihood of survival of a species or population, not of individuals. If a human individual succeeds in doing something or lives to a ripe old age, it is a mistake to conclude that the individual has adapted better than the rest of us and that we should all emulate his or her way of doing things. People live to a ripe old age not only because of what they themselves do, but also because other people teach them skills they need, because other people develop medicines for them, and so on. Our competence and longevity depend heavily on the social group and the population, not merely on ourselves as individuals. If a young man who has sired no children sacrifices his life so that the rest of us may live, should we say that we want to eliminate such people from our society, because the fact that they die before passing on their genes shows that they are not fit? With that, I have hinted at the next topic: the unit of diversity.

## The Unit of Diversity

We can think better about how to go about enhancing adaptability if we think about what unit ought to be the unit of diversity. That is, within what kind of unit should we strive to increase or maintain variety – individuals, groups, schools, districts, provinces, regions, or nations? My answer is: all of those.

Biologically, the individual does not exhibit diversity. Biologically, an individual differs from other individuals, but not from itself. It gets its genetic endowment at conception and never afterward gets anything different. Its genotype, in others words, never changes.

The individual's phenotype, however, does change. Our bodies change as we go from one diet or atmosphere to another and as we grow older. Socially, we change even more. Our interpersonal behaviour differs not only with age, but with the social roles we find ourselves in, with education, with travel, with having experienced happiness and grief, and so on. Through experience and education, it is possible to increase the diversity within an individual – that is, to increase the individual's flexibility and versatility. To put it in still other words, we can increase the repertoire of behaviour the individual can draw upon to deal with environmental events.

The same remarks apply to the other units – groups, schools, and so on. But social groups are even more plastic than individuals, because even their original design can be altered. An organization gets its original shape and purpose from its charter or constitution (in analogy to the individual's gene-pattern), but that charter or constitution can be amended or even ignored – and often is.

Let us now ask: If we want to make available to a school (for example) a greater variety of ways of doing things, what is the best unit among which to encourage differences? If we want to expand the pool of variety for schools, would it be better to increase differences among schools, or differences among groups within the school, or differences among districts, or what?

But for contrast, let us recall that biology gives only one answer. The biological adaptive unit is the population, and diversity is available to the population through the differences among individuals. If there is communication (interbreeding) between populations, then diversity can come from differences among individuals in an entire species. But one species cannot use individuals of another species as a source of diversity. Diversity resides in the population of a particular species.

Furthermore, a population changes, biologically, only by producing a different assortment of new individuals. It cannot alter its assortment of genes, its assortment in being, in any other way than through producing new individuals and therefore a new assortment of individuals.

Social adaptation does not work that way. An individual can alter its assortment of adaptive behaviour without producing a new leg, a new heart, or other part, and without waiting for progeny. The changes are produced through communication and influence. Some people would say the changes can also be produced through an act of will. That is a philosophical matter I shall not get into here.

Just as biological change depends on ease of access of one individual to another for purposes of mating, so social change depends on access to communication and influence. For that reason, I don't think we can provide schools with an easily available pool of variety by encouraging difference between nations (for example) in the ways they manage their educational systems.

Using the criterion of ease of access, I offer the hypothesis that the closer Unit Bs are to Unit A, the easier it will be for Unit A to select a new way of doing things from the variety among Unit Bs. For example, if a school is looking for a new way of doing things, it will be easier to borrow an idea from another school (and easier from close schools than from distant ones), somewhat harder to borrow from another district, harder yet to borrow from another province, and so on. And it will be easier for the school to borrow an idea from a group within itself than from an individual within itself – always excepting the principal.

Similarly, it will be easier for a team of teachers to borrow a way of doing things from another team in the same school or from an individual in the same school, harder to borrow one from a school as a whole, harder from the district, and so on.

Humans are very clever creatures; they can pick up ideas from anywhere. School administrators, for example, borrow ideas about administration from industrial firms. That example might seem to go contrary to my hypothesis about getting ideas most easily from near and similar units. But I am not saying that getting useful ideas from distant or dissimilar units is impossible. I am only saying, other things being equal, that it is easier to adopt ways of doing things from near and similar units than from distant and dissimilar ones.

To have diversity readily available, then, different ways of doing things should be going on from one teacher to another, from one teaching team or department to another, from one district to another, from one province to another, and from one nation to another. As circumstances change, we can then observe which teachers, teams, schools, and so on are dealing the more suitably with the new circumstances. But I don't mean that all other teachers, teams, schools, and so on should immediately imitate those that seem to be dealing best with the new circumstances. Some should and some should not. Some should stubbornly go on doing things they think will work best not perhaps in the present circumstances, but in circumstances they anticipate – circumstances they think will come about before long. Diversity should also be maintained to anticipate the future. Diversity should also be maintained because it is easy to be wrong about how well some way of doing things is working. The history of education is full of cases in which some new way of doing things – teaching machines, for example – looked very good at first, but then not very good later.

## Introducing Diversity

What can we do to make schooling more diverse than it is? The form for answering that question is simple: look for uniformity and then break it up. For example, perhaps we should have compulsory education in some places and not in others. Perhaps some districts should have school buildings and others should not. Perhaps in some places or in some classes students should do a lot of teaching. Perhaps there should be no principals in some schools. Perhaps some schools should operate without clocks. Perhaps some provinces or districts should do without prescribed curricula. Perhaps some teachers should get paid by the month and others by the student. Perhaps some students should study along with age-mates and others in groups of mixed ages. Perhaps students should study some subjects individually and others in cooperative workgroups. Perhaps some classrooms should be very quiet and others very noisy. It is easy to think of further possibilities. I leave it to the reader, as an exercise, to think of a hundred more ways to introduce variety into schooling.

If variety is to serve as insurance, it must be accessible, retrievable. If a teacher or school is doing something differently from others, it must be possible for others to learn about it. Good communication channels must exist.

Some communication channels already exist, but at present they serve chiefly the norm of uniformity. When one parent talks to another, for example, and they discover that their children are being taught different things or by different methods, both are likely to worry, each thinking that his or her child is getting something sub-standard. If diversity were commonplace, different would not have to imply inferior. If diversity were commonplace, parents would spread the news but not the worry when they talked about their children. Teachers would spread the news without being resented when they moved from one school to another.

More systematic communication networks can also be used. I mentioned earlier the National Diffusion Network supported by the US Office of Education. Several kinds of consultants to schools participate in their own formal and informal networks. In addition, school districts can organize some of their personnel to bring non-routine ideas to bear on problems arising in the schools of their district. I shall now describe a special kind of group that can support diversity in a school district – the Cadre of Organizational Specialists.

## The Cadre of Organizational Specialists

Communication is necessary if diversity is to be useful, but communication is not enough. The reason is that norms are not easy to change.

Every organization, every school, must observe a certain amount of routine if it is to operate from day to day. A routine is a kind of norm; it is maintained by sanctions. If it is necessary for all teachers to begin teaching at 8:30 in the morning, people who work at the school will speak approvingly to teachers who arrive on time and disapprovingly to those who do not. Some customs and routines are enforced with much more severe sanctions, such as dismissal.

The insidious thing about routine is that you get very little reward for conforming to it, but you usually get promptly punished for not conforming. The result is that contemplating a change in routine is always scary. People always do a lot of talking before they actually change some way of doing things in a school. One reason for all that talking is that Person A is busy extracting from Person B a promise that Person B will show approval, not disapproval, when Person A takes this step or that step toward doing things in the new way. And every Person A is trying to get those promises about all those steps from all those Person Bs. Sometimes, and for many reasons, those promises are hard to get.

People in a school or district can often make the necessary promises to one another more easily and more confidently with the help of a consultant from outside their own group. Richard Schmuck, several other colleagues, and I have tried out an organizational design for making consultants readily available to schools facing change. We call our design the Cadre of Organizational Specialists. (For descriptions, see Chapter two of Runkel, Wyant, Bell, and Runkel, 1980, and Chapter twelve of Schmuck, Runkel, Arends, and Arends, 1977.)

A Cadre of Organizational Specialists is a collegial group within a school district that helps groups facing change to focus their energies on the task and to generate the necessary trust that they will keep their promises to one another as they take the risky steps of change. A cadre helps with changes in roles, duties, interpersonal relations, coordination, communication, and the like. It helps increase the likelihood that a solution to a problem will 'stick' by building the solution with the people who will carry it out.

Here is our prescription for a cadre of organizational specialists. (1) Draw members from all ranks and from throughout the school district. Existing cadres have drawn from the following, in order from larger to smaller numbers: teachers, counsellors, principals and assistant principals, central-office specialists, assistant superintendents, secretaries, and parents. Applicants are typically screened to have had some professional experience in group dynamics and a favourable reputation in the district for knowledgeability and reliability. (2) Assign members part-time to the cadre – perhaps ten to twenty percent of their time. (3) Provide services by teams drawn from the cadre, rarely by individuals. (4) Do not impose cadre services; let the cadre respond to requests. The cadre should, however, advertise and give demonstrations. (5) Plan at least three weeks of training for cadre members, with appropriate followup consultation. (6) Do not assign cadre members to consult with the units in which they are regularly employed. (7) Appoint a Coordinator of the cadre, at least half time. (8) See that the cadre has at least ten active members. A couple of dozen is better. (9) Give the cadre its own budget. (10) Provide time for the cadre's own self-renewal: recruiting and training new members, acquiring new skills, renewing its own cohesiveness, planning for the future.

Since Richard Schmuck and I, with the help of several skilful colleagues, brought two cadres into being in the states of Washington and Oregon, several others have sprung up with only a very little consultation from us: three in California and one each in Colorado, Florida, New York, and Manitoba. The oldest one has now been thriving for nine years. They have helped schools with desegregation, curricular change, reduction of staff because of reduced enrolments, and a great variety of other changes and problems. They use ways of doing things that they find in being in their own district, they scout ways of doing things elsewhere, and they occasionally look into printed sources. In short, they serve as communicators, brokers, and trainers in diversity.

## Summary

I have said that I am convinced that our society is about to put unprecedented demands on our adaptability. To think about how we might improve our adaptability, I turned to biological diversity as an analogy. The important idea there is that we can insure ourselves against the stresses of unforeseen change by maintaining diversity in being.

To be ready to cope with change in the society, I said that we should do five things with schools:

1 Deliberately maintain diversity in the way we do things in schools.

2 Maintain the pool of variety (diversity) by maintaining actual deviant practices.

3 Establish conscious procedures for selecting the most suitable ideas for use in dealing with current problems. But we should not suppose that an idea most suitable for one school at one time is most suitable for every school at that time. Nor should we suppose that what is most suitable for one school today will be most suitable for it tomorrow.

4 Build channels to more parts of the school environment through which information and influence can reach the school. Try especially to reach minority cultures.

5 Accept the discomfort, anxiety, and even fear that comes from harbouring deviance. Accept it as the price, and the bargain price, of adaptability.

I urged that we encourage diversity at all levels: individual, group, school, district, province and nation. I pointed out that using diversity requires good communication, and I mentioned an example or two of communication networks that can be used. Finally, I said that using diversity requires social support. I described the Cadre of Organizational Specialists as one way to provide it.

I have no doubt that we shall adapt, one way or another. Humans are astonishingly adaptable. I have taken time to propose some deliberate ways to enhance the adaptability of our schools, however, because I hope that we can be ready to maintain some continuity with the past and to select new forms for the future with a minimum of painful disruption.

## References

ALSCHULER, A., ATKINS, S., IRONS, R.B., MULLEN, R.M. and SORTIAGO-WOLTOW, N. (1977) 'Collaborative problem solving as an aim of education in a democracy: The social literacy project' *Journal of Applied Behavioral Science* 13 pp. 305–327.

ANDERSON, C.H. (1976) *The Sociology of Survival: Social Problems of Growth* Homewood, Ill., Dorsey Press.

APPLEY. D.G. and WINDER, A. (Issue Eds.) (1977) 'Collaboration in work settings' *Journal of Applied Behavioral Science* 13(3).

ARGYRIS, C. and SCHON, D.A. (1974) *Theory in Practice: Increasing Professional Effectiveness* San Francisco, Jossey-Bass.

BOWLES, S. and GINTIS, H. (1976) *Schooling in Capitalist America: Educa-*

*tional Reform and the Contradictions of Economic Life* New York, Basic Books.

BUCKLEY, W. (1967) *Sociology and Modern Systems Theory* Englewood Cliffs, N.J., Prentice-Hall.

COLEMAN, J.S. (1972) 'The children have outgrown the schools' *Psychology Today* 5(9) pp. 72–82.

DAVIS, L.E. and CHERNS, A.B. (Eds) *The Quality of Working Life* Vol. 1 New York, Free Press.

DECI, E.L. (1972) 'Work – who does not like it and why' *Psychology Today* 6(3) pp. 57–92.

EHRLICH, P.R. (1979) Diversity and the steady state. Winner of the Mitchell Prize at the Woodlands Conference on Growth Policy, Houston, Tex.

ELGIN, D.S. and BUSHNELL, R.A. (1977) 'The limits to complexity: Are bureaucracies becoming unmanageable? *Futurist* 11(6) pp. 337–349.

ELGIN, D.S. and MITCHELL, A. (1977) 'Voluntary simplicity' (3) *CoEvolution Quarterly* Summer pp. 4–19.

FREIRE, P. (1972) *The Pedagogy of the Oppressed* New York, Herder and Herder.

HEDBERG, B.L.T., NYSTROM, P.C. and STARBUCH, W.H. (1976) 'Camping on seesaws: Prescriptions for a self-designing organization' *Administrative Science Quarterly* 21(1) pp. 41–65.

HESPE, G. and WALL, T. (1976) 'The demand for participation among employees' *Human Relations* 29(5) pp. 411–428.

*ISR Newsletter* (1977) 'Experiments show employees can determine their own wages, fringe benefits, and work policies' 5(3) pp. 3–6.

KAUFMANN, F. (1979) 'The jobs that nobody wants: Economic challenges of the 1980s' *Futurist* August pp. 269–274.

MEYER, J. and ROWAN, B. (1977) 'Institutionalized organizations: Formal structure as myth and ceremony' *American Journal of Sociology* 83(2) pp. 340–363.

RUNKEL, P.J., SCHMUCK, R.A., ARENDS, J.H. and FRANCISCO, R.P. (1979) *Transforming the School's Capacity for Problem Solving* Eugene, Ore., Center for Educational Policy and Management.

RUNKEL, P.J., WYANT, S.H., BELL, W.E. and RUNKEL, M. (1980) *Organizational Renewal in a School District: Self-help through a Cadre of Organizational Specialists* Eugene, Ore., Center for Educational Policy and Management.

SCHMUCK, R.A., RUNKEL, P.J., ARENDS, J.H. and ARENDS, R.I. (1977) *The Second Handbook of Organization Development in Schools* Palo Alto, Calif., Mayfield.

SCHUMACHER, E.F. (1979) *Good Work* New York, Harper and Row.

SMITH, W.A. *The Meaning of Conscientizacao: The Goal of Paulo Freire's Pedagogy* Amherst, Mass., Center for International Education, University of Massachusetts.

STAVRIANOS, L.S. (1976) *The Promise of the Coming Dark Age* San Francisco, W.H. Freeman.

STOBAUGH, R. and YERGIN, D. (Eds.) (1979) *Energy Future: The Report of the Energy Project at the Harvard Business School* New York, Random House.

WEICK, K.E. (1979) *The Social Psychology of Organizing* 2nd ed. Reading, Mass., Addison-Wesley.

WEIZENBAUM, J. (1976) *Computer Power and Human Reason: From Judgment to Calculation* San Francisco, W.H. Freeman.

ZWERDLING, D. (1979) *Workplace Democracy: A Guide to Workplace Ownership, Participation, and Self-management: Experiments in the United States and Europe* New York, Harper and Row.

# *Implications for Practice*

Marvin F. Wideen and Ian Andrews
Simon Fraser University

## Introduction

The papers in this book have offered an alternative perspective on school improvement to those programme initiatives that have prevailed in most parts of North America and Western Europe during the past several decades. Previous attempts to improve the schools have taught us that for innovation to effect instruction and learning in classrooms implementation strategies are required. By including a chapter that considers the implications of the previous chapters, we hope that the ideas addressed in this book can be placed one step closer to the practical realities of the classroom or school.

We have read and reread the papers that make up this book seeking to draw out the major implications for three specific categories of educators. One category includes those individuals who work in classrooms and in schools; the second includes those who plan in-service education and implement curriculum; and, the third category, those who develop and implement academic and administrative policy aimed at improving the quality of schooling. We have tried to draw meaning from each chapter in terms of improving the quality of schooling. Also, we have pondered on how teachers and support personnel might think through the book in order to draw out implications that may apply to their own professional jurisdiction. We invite you to engage in a similar undertaking. What follows is our analysis resulting from that process.

Two disclaimers are necessary before turning to the implications as such. To illustrate the first disclaimer allow us to cite the story of the writer who was asked how to rid the Atlantic ocean of submarines. His reply was simple,

'Raise the ocean to boiling point.'
'But that's not practical, you would kill the fish and at any

rate how could you do it!' was the reply.

'You only asked me for a solution,' replied the writer,' 'not a practical one.'

We often hear of simple solutions to the problems facing the schools. The idea of deschooling society or prophesying a revolution in the schools are about as absurd as raising the ocean to boiling point. Schools are here to stay (at least for the foreseeable future) and so are teachers; if a revolution is going to occur in the schools, it will take time – so much time that we may not even notice it. Our disclaimer is this. Although the implications of the concepts described in these papers can be seen as revolutionary in scope, we believe that a revolution is not required to have these ideas manifest in our schools. Hence the discussion that follows is not based on the assumption that a revolution is to occur, or that schools will be radically different this time next year.

Second, it is not our intent to replace dogma with dogma or to create yet another orthodoxy. Clearly, this book provides an alternative perspective but it makes no claim to be the only perspective that can form the basis of change in education. Rather, we propose a set of different ways of looking at schools which we think are likely to be very powerful in turning them into better places for quality teaching and learning to occur.

Therefore in this chapter we focus on the starting points, the steps to take, and the new perspectives that are likely to be instrumental in creating better schools. As such, we invite the reader to become engaged in the critical reflection that Aoki describes as a process that expects educators to analyze the assumptions and intentions of their professional beliefs and actions.

We begin by identifying themes that ran through the twelve previous chapters. Those themes culminate in a new perspective or paradigm for school improvement, which we describe in the second section. We then examine the levels of application of this paradigm and conclude by reflecting upon some issues that emanate from this approach.

## Themes

Four themes emerged from our study of the book:

1 the need for increased awareness,
2 the need to actively support and facilitate but not control,

3 the need to understand the complexity of the process, and
4 the need for diversity.

*Increased awareness*

The need for increased awareness about the many aspects of school improvement on the part of all concerned is the first theme that permeates previous sections and one which offers the first step towards implementation. If we enter the task of school improvement assuming that in the past we have not succeeded dramatically in our attempts, we spare ourselves the disappointment of high expectations not being fulfilled. As Ekholm shows us in Section One, where he relates the Swedish experience, improvements come slowly even under conditions which are near ideal. On the positive side of our past experience is the recognition that much has been learned about school improvement and that the task can now be greatly enhanced if those involved become more aware of that knowledge. Teachers need to be more aware of the political situation and conceptual frameworks in which they operate. It is alarming to discover that many teachers feel professionally constrained; yet upon examination those constraints are found to be imposed by their own perceptions. Teachers must become aware of the latitude they could enjoy and of the great amount of institutional flexibility that exists in most jurisdictions. It is within such institutional flexibility that many of the ideas proposed in this book can be applied.

Planners of in-service could improve what they do by showing a greater awareness that top down models of school improvement have been ineffective. Researchers, too, need to be mindful that school improvement has been poorly informed by research largely because of inappropriate paradigms. The typical experimental and quasi-experimental studies reported in academic journals bear little relationship to the reality of most classrooms nor do they speak a language that can be understood by most practitioners.

Being aware is sometimes little more than knowing one's history and being sensitive to its messages. School improvement has a history that began when the schools began. Much is known about what works and what does not work. In recent years, as Hopkins noted in the opening chapter, increasing efforts have been made to record what is known. A useful starting point for any jurisdiction (school or district) would be to step back from their immediate situation and to consider this accumulated wisdom. But history goes beyond that which is recorded in educational books, journals and magazines. It also includes the personal experience of a teacher and the collective experience which we call a school. This part of history must also be taken into account or we will simply repeat the errors of the past.

## *The need to support, facilitate, but not control*

Implied throughout this book, is the concept of a teacher free to initiate, plan and implement new ideas while being encouraged to accomplish these tasks with limited constraint or control from outside. Stenhouse's ideal of the teacher as artist is unlikely to develop in a tightly controlled system. As he suggests, the teacher must be allowed the opportunity to exercise autonomy of judgement. Similarly, Aoki's concept of critical analysis requires room to function. He proposes that teachers be liberated to pursue actions that would critically reflect upon and make adjustments to their practice. The challenge will be to provide such freedom within the constraints imposed by local, state, provincial and national jurisdictions. Frequently, policy makers far removed from the problems of the classroom legislate in ways that dictate what teachers do. Certainly such central bodies have legitimate roles in developing policy. However, such policy must be developed so that it facilitates and supports activities in schools rather than controlling or directing them. Also, changes required by new policies must be communicated effectively to teachers. Perhaps of most importance in the interface between policy makers and teachers are those in positions of middle management. It is they who can support, initiate and bring about effective implementation because, without such support, teachers cannot be expected to achieve effective change – the task is simply too immense.

By identifying this particular theme, we are not suggesting that those who make policy, and those who provide resources adopt a *laissez-faire* attitude toward the schools. The conclusion drawn by Ekholm from the Swedish experience was that it is necessary for outside persons to be involved in the school for purpose of diagnosis and stimulation so that a school staff can reach its aims. The Australian experience as reported by Eltis and his colleagues was similar where the role of tertiary personnel was found to be a necessary condition for effective activity within the school.

What appears to be necessary in this regard is the finding of an appropriate blend of activity from within the school coupled with support and expertise from outside needed to facilitate the process. But as we pointed out earlier, within that negotiated blend, sufficient freedom for teachers to approach changes in their own way must be provided.

## The Complexity of the Process

Clearly evident in Joyce and Showers' paper on coaching and emphasized by Runkel is the recurrent theme of complexity. [During the Summer Institute on Teacher Education (described in the introduction) Runkel presented a paper, 'Humans as Social Animals'. He carefully detailed how the complexity of any social system increases as more people become involved in an activity.] People are complex animals and as Runkel points out, the more people involved, the more complex the process becomes. Added to this complexity are the many variables which affect any social system such as a school. The term school improvement itself can imply many things ranging from the introduction of new curriculum and technology, in-service education for teachers, or the introduction of consultants into the system. Irrespective of the type of innovation, its introduction is complex. While the literature on change and implementation has provided a great deal of insight and results, it is largely silent on how the many variables and complexities can best be managed. We have considered inputs and outputs but rarely studied the black box in the middle. In fact, it is not entirely clear what the black box is. Is it the teacher, the classroom, the school, or the system? The complexity question virtually rules out the faint hope that tinkering with the system, unfortunately evident in much current in-service and curriculum development programming, will have any effect. It also underlines the importance of time in achieving results and probably encourages us again to seek small but substantial beginnings rather than massive superficial organizational programme changes.

## The Need for Diversity

In the previous chapter Runkel compares schools to a biological system evolving through diversity. He argues that the need exists in education for greater diversity that will produce alternative approaches, some of which will be more effective than standard practices. Other papers in this book pick up this theme. Joyce, for example, in his SITE lecture discussed the need for more wild-eyed crazies, those teachers who are willing to undertake exciting and challenging innovations. Stenhouse envisages autonomous teachers seeking change and growth through artistry. The theme is simply that the acceptance of diversity is necessary for change and school improvement. It is through such diversity that natural experiments can occur which exemplify better practices. Another argument for diversity is that it maximizes the potential of teachers because it caters to the talents within each individual. Just as the concept of individuality has been recognized in children, so must the concept be recognized in teachers. If we assume that school improvement can best be achieved through enhancing the contribution of every teacher, then the recognition of individual differences among teachers becomes crucially important. Part of this diversity also is the recognition that for many teachers exercising individuality may not be effective; for them, adherence to accepted practice may be the most appropriate.

A further argument for diversity arises out of the complexity of the process. It is highly unlikely, if not impossible, to assume that the type of school improvement discussed in these papers is possible on a grand scale. It is unlikely that a school district, for example, could ever implement in every school the kind of improvement efforts discussed in this book. We simply do not know enough to accomplish such a feat. What is more feasible is the broken front approach, where individuals are encouraged to review their practice, identify remedies and pursue appropriate strategies. Recognition by school administrators of the value of this professional freedom among teachers will ensure that diversity is encouraged. But recognition of diversity is not, of itself, sufficient to nurture it. Frequently, the need is for administrators to provide shelter conditions for certain projects to flourish and develop.

The discussion now turns to the implications of these themes at the level of the classroom, the teacher, the school, and the supporting agencies.

## The Culture of the Classroom

We begin with the assumption that school improvement will require changes in classrooms which affect both the culture of the classroom and the role of the teacher. [We see the culture of the classroom as that set of ideals and beliefs that are developed and which maintain a certain set of expectations about life and learning within the classroom.]

Rudduck's premise that pupils must be considered in the implementation process brings into sharp focus the need for teachers and educational planners to recognize the culture of the classroom as being influential in determining the success of an innovation. What does such a recognition imply for school improvement? First it requires that teachers who innovate must be aware that a culture exists in their classroom that may have to be 'deprogrammed' before a new approach is introduced. In many cases, new skills or changes in roles may be required of both the teacher and the students. As Rudduck describes, the introduction of innovation among pupils often causes problems of disorientation and uncertainty. The realization by the pupils that the regular pattern of instruction or classroom programming is changing can cause much dissonance and anxiety. Hence, teachers need to describe to students what the change is about and specify clearly what new skills and role changes are required. Rudduck further argues that negotiation is required between teacher and student about such new roles and the requirement of new learning environments.

Of most importance in this regard is the need for cooperation between student and teacher in a type of 'communal venturing' as described by Aoki in his chapter on curriculum implementation. He suggests that opportunity for students to interact with the teacher in their own language about new ideas or innovations in curriculum content or instructional methodology is crucial. This allows the reciprocity of joint critical reflection and common discovery to manifest itself. A common respect and trust will be enhanced by both teacher and pupils as they seek a mutual understanding of the classroom innovation. As Aoki affirms, the process of implementation is therefore 'constituted by the inter-subjective actions of beings-as-humans'.

What we have just said with regard to how teachers react with students applies equally to others who in one way or another plan for school improvement. Those who develop curricula, for example, need to plan for the students' role changes.

### The teacher

One perspective that affirms the need for the teacher to reconceptualize his/her role in the classroom is described in Stenhouse's chapter 'Artistry and Teaching'. The teacher is described as an artist in terms of his/her ability to convey the structure of subject matter to students. One may interpret the status of the teacher as artist by using the guild system analogy that sees the individual evolve from an apprentice to a journeyman to a craftsman to a master artist. As in the guild system the teacher evolves through experience and exhibits skills and knowledge comparable to these stages, possibly reaching the master teacher status over time. At the artistry stage the teacher seeks further understanding by utilizing as an art form research to improve teaching. The teacher is seen here as an active conceptualist operating through critical analysis to further his or her own development. School improvement arises, according to Stenhouse, through this search for truth. He further argues that like the artist, the teacher must eventually move into the arena where the art form (teaching) is held up to the scrutiny of others.

This orientation implies that teachers require a freedom within their classroom to innovate and to pursue curriculum development or instructional planning. This 'adventure in education' provides an excitement and positive spirit that can enhance the professional development of the teacher. This complements Stenhouse's belief that good teachers are necessarily autonomous in professional judgment. As we shall discuss, the support system personnel must respect the teacher's judgment but also ensure the teacher can seek change and innovation with the necessary reinforcement and not be impeded by unnecessary intervention. Inquiry of thought and action is not complemented by a repressive or restrictive environment.

If we juxtapose the propositions of Rudduck and Stenhouse with Aoki's concept of critical analysis and communal venturing a new role for the teacher emerges. Teaching then becomes the object of inquiry and reflection and the improvement of teaching the goal. The teacher now becomes the inquirer, and the classroom a laboratory in which techniques and new ideas are constantly being tested and practices continually being examined to discover the hidden assumptions and motives underlying them. The obvious implications for teachers is to begin thinking as a professional who extends beyond the journeyman and craftsman to become a master teacher. The distinction involves a change in perception as well as additional training and the acquisition of new skills. In fact, the change in perception must precede the acquisition of new knowledge or skills. The first step for the teacher is to view his/her teaching as a practice to be studied, evaluated, or improved. Eventually, the quest by the teacher for further skills, new knowledge, and outside help will be pursued.

## The School

The writings of Lortie (1975) and Sarason (1971) have suggested that initiatives within classrooms are unlikely to have lasting impact without complementary efforts at the school level. In fact, much of the current literature on in-service points to the need for the school to be the focus for change. However, moving to the level of the school brings with it increased complexities, as was shown earlier, simply because of the involvement of more people, more contacts, and so on. Fortunately, organizational development strategies are available which can resolve many implementation problems at a school level. The steps provided by Runkel and Schmuck have been successfully used in many jurisdictions, as have procedures outlined by Eltis and his colleagues which resulted from their experience in Australia. Several implications emerge from their papers regarding the role of the school in the improvement of educational practice. These include the need for leadership within the school, the need for outside support and expertise, the need for time and resources to be available and, as described earlier, the appreciation of the complexity of the task, the need for accepting diversity, as well as the need to change perceptions.

If the autonomous school, with its democratic style is to characterize our education system, then as Schmuck suggests, the school's capacity for problem solving will be enhance. And as Runkel postulates, institutionalizing changes in the school environment will only succeed when continual analysis of the change process is made by the participants. Similarly the teacher must be afforded professional development opportunities so that they can learn the nature of the innovation or institutionalized change.

If teaching is to emerge as an art form with the teacher as an inquirer into his/her own teaching, then the school must play a supportive role in two ways. First, it must legitimize the activity and provide shelter conditions particularly at the early stages of innovation. It is through the legitimization of the teacher as researcher at the school level, that teachers will begin to venture forth into the unchartered territory of inquiry and risk-taking. This involvement takes place when teachers begin to examine their own practice and to probe their assumptions. However, legitimization must be followed by the sheltering of those new ventures on which teachers and students need to embark if the notion of teacher as researcher is to achieve viability. Both will require a certain type of leadership at the school level which not only provides support but demonstrate a willingness to foster experimentation. Clearly, a certain type of leadership is required, reflecting neither the paternalistic nor *laissez-faire* position so prevalent in schools today. As Schmuck suggests, the democratic leader must distribute power throughout the staff, using his/her authority to ensure that decision making influence is attained by all staff members.

Principals must endeavour to gain a cognitive grasp of the innovation that the teacher is implementing in the classroom. The leaders in the school must assist the teacher to actualize the realities of the teacher's aspirations. Not always will the principal totally agree with the specifics of the innovative programme, yet, if the energy and commitment of the teacher is to be maximized, then the principal must shelter the teacher's venture and attempt to extend the teacher's strengths and talents when they are undertaking the projects. Passive support or total indifference by the principal does not assist teachers in helping them to achieve their goals. There is a need for positive and active endorsement.

## Supporting Agencies

A clear implication of much of what has been said is the need for outside support. Joyce's work has demonstrated that teachers are very capable of learning new models of teaching and of refining skills, but implied is the need for assistance to do both. It is unlikely that the talent to provide all the skills are present in the school itself. Similarly the application of organization development at the school level usually requires an outside person to introduce the concepts of organization development. One could go on with numerous examples. The point is, that the complexities of the task and the skills that need to be brought to bear on the situation are such that in many cases we must look beyond the school. This is the main point of departure between what underlies many of the chapters in this volume and the notion of school based in-service or curriculum development which focuses primarily on the school staff as the source. Nevertheless, it is crucial that whatever outside support is introduced the teachers must initiate, examine and engage openly with the consulting personnel.

Throughout, we have talked about the complexity of the process and the need for concerted action planning to make significant school improvement feasible. Both time and resources are required to achieve significant improvement. Time is necessary to think, plan, act and to see the fruits of the endeavour. Resources are required to support the time needed by teachers as well as to maximize the outside expertise that is necessary. Infrequent visits or superficial support by outside personnel will not suffice. They must become collaborators who demonstrate a willingness to support and invest their commitment to the project.

The onus for much of the change that is necessary lies with the principal of the school. Fullan's chapter addresses the ideal in this regard. But contrasting that ideal with current practice finds a wide dichotomy. Just as we said that teachers first needed to change their perceptions about classrooms, we now argue that principals and senior staff must do the same. The type of critical analysis about which Aoki speaks can occur in a school as well as at the classroom level. The teachers as researchers could be rephrased as the principal as a researcher. Indeed, perhaps that is where it should start. The role of research and evaluation have most frequently been seen as outside activities, conducted by outside agencies. Throughout these chapters we have seen the potential for a much different type of activity coming under the aegis of evaluation and research. In Robinson's chapter the notion of a school review is described as a means of contributing to the improvement of the school. Similarly we have referred to research throughout as an activity carried out much closer to the school and classroom. We believe that such activity is much more likely to inform the process of school improvement than efforts of the past.

Planners and developers must also become more aware of the culture of the schools and classrooms they hope to change. Similarly they must become aware of the demands being placed upon the recipient (both teachers and students) of such changes. Awareness must also apply to the complexity of the task.

Planners and developers will also have to deal with certain issues likely to arise through increased collaboration. First, they should review what has been said in the political context of their own jurisdiction. They might further ask what purposes are currently being served through various school improvement programmes. Are their efforts likely to be improved through taking certain of the steps we are proposing? Perhaps one of the most important questions to consider during this stage of critical analysis is the cultural problem to which we referred earlier. Can a group of planners recognize and deal with the prospect that, much like the schools they intend to change, they have themselves become trapped into the cultural inertia of past decades. Recognition of that is one step, changing it is another.

Research needs to be conducted which will produce effective models of staff development which in turn need to be subjected to rigorous testing. A preliminary step to such development will be descriptive sociological studies that provide insight into how schools function. Without such information it is difficult to know how we can propose improved models of staff development. The procedures used would do well to make greater use of teachers as full partners rather than subjects and the use of the results must be fed back to schools in ways that provide insight and awareness to the participants involved.

## Implications of Transition

It is difficult to conceive of a complete transition from what appears to be the current mode of educational thinking to the alternative proposed here in the short term. What appears to be more fruitful is to think in terms of stages partly temporal and partly conceptual and then to consider the implications at each stage.

For example, the first stage of transition is that of awareness. As argued throughout this book, a predominant mode of thinking pervades most efforts aimed at school improvement. Aoki has described this theme as instrumental action in which implementation involves the installation of curriculum, the success of which is judged by the fidelity of the installed curriculum compared with that of the original plan. In this orientation, curriculum development is a process for experts and the subjectivity of the teacher is irrelevant, if not problematic. Supporting groups, teachers and principals need to become aware that this approach has serious shortcomings and is being questioned by the very people who proposed the underlying model.

Creating awareness of the existing paradigms and alternatives to them is of limited value in improving our schools if critical reflection does not occur and action follow. Let us continue using the example of instrumental action as the predominant mode of implementation. To be aware of its existence is a first step; but uncritically adopting an alternative simply replaces dogma with dogma. It is not our contention that instrumental action has no role in school improvement. We do contend that it has substantial limitations which require examination in the light of alternatives which have been shown to be more effective and within the context of local jurisdictions.

It is from this analysis that action plans follow. As we have argued throughout, the process is complex and is likely to be more effective where small, successful first steps are taken rather than massive attempts which tend to be ineffective because of their remote and superficial nature.

## Summary

Our chapter set out to draw implications for school improvement emanating from the other chapters in the book. We first identified four themes: the need for awareness, the need to support and facilitate but not control complexity and the need for diversity. These themes were explored at the level of the classroom, school and supporting agencies where the emphasis was upon examining current practice, exploring alternatives, and proposing action plans. Also, the need for collaboration and joint planning were emphasized where the culture of the school, the needs of the system, and the potential of the teacher coalesce in the search for better schools.

## References

LORTIE, D.C. (1975) *School Teacher: A Sociological Study* Chicago, University of Chicago Press.

SARASON, S.B. (1971) *The Culture of the School and the Problem of Change* Boston, Allyn and Bacon.

# *Contributors*

**Ian Andrews** is assistant director of professional programs in the Faculty of Education at Simon Fraser University. As such he has been responsible for the implementation of one of Canada's most innovative teacher education programs. He is currently engaged on doctoral research which focuses on the confluence of pre-service and in-service teacher education programs as it applies to the delivery of services and programs to beginning teachers.

**Ted Aoki** is chairman of the Department of Secondary Education in the Faculty of Education, University of Alberta. His work in curriculum theorizing and evaluation is widely known throughout Canada, and he has made a substantial contribution to the popularization of critical theory in North America.

**John Braithwaite** is a Senior Lecturer in Education at Macquarie, with teaching and research interests in curriculum studies and programme evaluation.

**Christine E. Deer** is a Senior Lecturer in Education at Macquarie University where she obtained her Ph.D. Her teaching and research interests include curriculum studies, school and home, and school and community relationships and organizational climate.

**Mats Ekholm** is the Director of the Swedish School Leader program supported by the National Board of Education in that country. In his position he directs several national projects. Previous to that he was a researcher at the University of Gothenburg working in the area of sociology of education. He has published extensively in the areas, of the social development of young people and the training of school principals.

**Ken Eltis** is Director of the Teacher Education Program at Macquarie

University. He was for a number of years co-ordinator of the practicum in the Teacher Education Programme and has done extensive work in the area of teaching skills development and the development of programmes to improve skills of practicum supervision. He co-ordinated the inservice project on which the present contribution is based.

**Michael Fullan** is an assistant director at the Ontario Institute for Studies in Education. His publications, particularly his work on curriculum implementation and *educational* change, have received international recognition. His recent book *The Meaning of Educational Change*, is published by the Teachers College Press and OISE Press.

**David Hopkins** is a lecturer in Educational Research at the West Glamorgan Institute of Higher Education in South Wales. He previously instructed at Simon Fraser University, where he co-directed the institute that led to this book. Currently, he is collaborating with Jean Rudduck on a book called *Research as a basis for teaching* that celebrates Lawrence Stenhouse's pioneering work. He divides his time between teacher education, writing and climbing mountains.

**Bruce Joyce** is an internationally known teacher educator who has published over 50 books, including the well known *Models of Teaching* (with Marsha Weil, Prentice Hall, 1980, 2nd edition). He is one of the most experienced large-scale educational researchers in North America, and is presently directing a research project on teacher effectiveness and school improvement for the State of California.

**Harry Kensell** is a Senior Lecturer in Education at Macquarie University. His teaching and research interests include teacher education, inservice education and organizational climate of schools.

**Viviane Robinson** is a Senior Lecturer in Education at the University of Auckland. She has developed and introduced courses for senior students in the analysis and improvement of organizational effectiveness, and also specializes in experiential training procedures for teaching job-related interpersonal and consultancy skills. She did her doctoral studies at Harvard University, and has published extensively, with her current emphasis being on the conditions within organizations that facilitate or inhibit their adaptation and change.

**Jean Rudduck** is a senior lecturer at the Centre for Applied Research in Education at the University of East Anglia. Since working on the Humanities Curriculum Project she has been responsible for a number of projects concerned with classroom research and curriculum change. She has written books on curriculum development and dissemination; small group learning; in-service activities; and teacher research.

**Philip Runkel** is a professor of education and psychology at the University of Oregon. He is one of America's leading social psychologists, and has published some ten books in that field. His fourteen year programme of research with Richard Schmuck on organizational change in school systems has brought him international recognition, which was recently consolidated by the publication of three books – *The Second Handbook of O.D. in Schools* (with Schmuck, Arends and Arends), *Transforming the School's Capacity for Problem Solving* (with Schmuck, Arends and Francisco) and *Organizational Renewal in a School District* (with Wyant, Bell and Runkel).

**Richard Schmuck** is a professor of education and psychology and Director of Graduate Studies in Educational Policy and Management at the University of Oregon. He has published thirteen books on the social psychology of education. Two of them, . . . *Organization Development in Schools* (with Matthew Miles), and *Group Processes in the Classroom* (with his wife Patricia Schmuck) are widely used by teachers, students, and administrators. Since 1967 he has collaborated with Philip Runkel on a programme of research and development on organizational change in schools. Their two books, *The Second Handbook of O.D. in Schools* and *Transforming the School's Capacity for Problem Solving*, have received wide and enthusiastic critical response.

**Beverly Showers** teaches at the University of Oregon. She has published a number of articles on teacher education and training, including the well known 'Improving Inservice Training: the messages of research' (with Bruce Joyce).

**Lawrence Stenhouse** was the director of the Centre for Applied Research in Education at the University of East Anglia. Prior to that he was director of the Humanities Curriculum Project and has published some five books including the seminal, *An Introduction to Curriculum Research and Development* (Heinemann, 1975). He was perhaps the most eloquent and sophisticated advocate of teacher based programmes of research and development. His recent death was a great personal and professional loss to us all.

**Marvin Wideen** is an associate professor of education at Simon Fraser University. He has recently co-directed (with Michael Fullan) a large scale research project on the management of change in teacher education in Canada, and is conducting an ongoing program of research into the professional development of teachers. He is currently working on a book, *Innovation and Change in Teacher Education: A Cross-Cultural Perspective.*

# Author Index

# Author Index

Weil, M.
  see Joyce and Weil
Weiss, I.B., 78, 87
Weizenbaum, J., 170, 187
Wellisch, W.A. et al., 95–6, 100, 103
Werner, W., 115, 118
White, R. and Lippitt, R., 27, 32
Whiteside, T., 141, 151
Wideen, M. and Andrews, I., 4, 165, 189–201
Wilen, W.W. and Kindsvatter, R., 80, 87
Winder, A.

  see Appley and Winder
Wohlleb, C.
  see Lukacs and Wohlleb
Wojtyla, K., 113–14, 118
Wolcott, H.F., 93–4, 103

Yergin, D.
  see Stobaugh and Yergin

Zakariya, S.
  see Pharis and Zakariya
Zwerdling, D., 170, 187